ANYTHING
THAT MOVES

RIVERHEAD BOOKS

A MEMBER OF PENGUIN GROUP (USA)

NEW YORK

2013

ANYTHING THAT MOVES

Renegade Chefs,

Fearless Eaters,

and the Making of

a New American

Food Culture

DANA GOODYEAR

RIVERHEAD BOOKS
Published by the Penguin Group
Penguin Group (USA) LLC
375 Hudson Street
New York, New York 10014

USA · Canada · UK · Ireland · Australia
New Zealand · India · South Africa · China

penguin.com
A Penguin Random House Company

Portions of this book have appeared in different form in *The New Yorker*.

Library of Congress Cataloging-in-Publication Data

Goodyear, Dana.
Anything that moves : renegade chefs, fearless eaters, and the making
of a new American food culture / Dana Goodyear.
p.   cm.
ISBN 978-1-59448-837-5
1. Food—Social aspects—United States.   2. Food habits—United States.
3. Cooking—Social aspects—United States.   4. Extremists—United States.
5. Cooks—United States.   6. Gourmets—United States.   7. United States—Social
life and customs—1971–   I. Title.
GT2853.U5G66   2013   2013025054
394.1'2—dc23

Printed in the United States of America
1   3   5   7   9   10   8   6   4   2

BOOK DESIGN BY AMANDA DEWEY

For Rummy and Willa, my darlings

CONTENTS

ANYTHING
THAT MOVES

INTRODUCTION

Bugs, horse, brains, whale; leaves, weeds, ice cream fla-vored with lichen-covered logs. The disturbingly famil-iar and the alarmingly rare, the unregulated, illegal, and indeterminate. A new American cuisine is forming, one marked by extreme and challenging ingredients. Animals never before considered or long since forgotten are emerging as delicacies. Parts that used to be for scrap are centerpieces. Ash and hay are fashionable ingredients, and you pay handsomely to breathe fla-vored air. I haven't yet heard of an American chef with the nerve to serve actual dirt—in Tokyo you can get a fancy dirt soup, and compost is an ingredient at one of Spain's most celebrated restaurants—but a high-end meal in this country feels incom-plete these days without a little mound of "soil" made from cocoa or coffee. Going out to a nice dinner often precipitates a confron-tation with a fundamental evolutionary question: Is that food?

My relationship to food is that of an acrophobe to a bridge: unease masks a desire to jump. A well-fed child with the imagination of a scrounger, I remember holing up in the back of the station wagon eating the dog's Milk-Bones, which were tastier than you might expect. Thinking of the sorrel that grew under our swing set still makes me drool. In winter—we lived outside Cleveland at that point—we drizzled maple syrup on the snow. My mother, who taught herself to cook by reading Elizabeth David, made everything from scratch, down to the English muffins. (She says I once asked her peevishly if it wouldn't be more convenient to buy some frozen food.) My father hunted. We always had a meat freezer full of doves from the eastern shore of Maryland and elk from the Rockies.

As I grew older, I remained curious. When I was in college, I got a summer job in Hong Kong at the *South China Morning Post*. After being teased in the lunchroom by a Singaporean colleague for being squeamish, I tried chicken feet. In Hanoi, I went to a dog restaurant and ate seven courses of "hornless goat." (Back home, I told my disgusted family that dogs may have been domesticated to serve as a source of meat in lean times. They still thought I was gross.) In Africa, I ate African animals; in South America, South American ones. But at home I was a "normal" eater—no chicken feet, no pets.

Until I started hanging out with foodies. Coined by the critic Gael Greene in 1980 to describe the devoted fans of an untrained Paris housewife who cooked in heels, the word *foodie* has taken on a new life in the age of social media. An American foodie documents what she eats with the avidity of a competitive birder, and publishes the images online for the world to see.

So-called food porn is the most popular content on Pinterest, one of the fastest-growing websites in history, and it dominates the photo-sharing sites Instagram and Flickr. It's everywhere on TV. And, as with any fetish, the more outlandish and rarefied a find, the more a foodie likes it.

In "The Food Wife," a 2011 episode of *The Simpsons*, Marge and the kids become thrill-seeking food bloggers, sampling pig snouts, walrus moustaches, pine-needle sorbet, and a "regret course" of human tears. Matthew Selman, who wrote the episode and considers it a love letter to his kind, arranges family trips around restaurant reservations and finds himself ordering "the most organy, taily, brainy, nosy thing in the world—*because* it's exciting and dangerous." He has a hard time with the terminology, though. "I wish there was a word other than 'foodie,'" he says. "How about 'super food asshole' or 'pretentious food jerk'?" But somehow this piggy, cute, overweening word is right. *Gourmet* is too grand—too faux—for this movement; *epicure* is too ancient. We needed a word in English—a keen, young, democratic word—to describe the epidemic of food love.

L ate-Roman eating habits are, to us, the emblem of the society's decadence, a forerunner of and justification for its fall. According to Patrick Faas, a historian of Roman food, "Rome became the giant stomach of the world, devouring everything," during its five hundred years of imperial rule. The rich considered birds' brains a delicacy and relished moray eels, which they kept in swimming pools at home. (Vedius Pollio, a friend of Augustus, supposedly preferred his eels fattened on human flesh.) In the third century AD, Emperor Elagabalus served coxcombs, peacock heads, and, as an accompaniment to womb-in wild sow, peas with gold, lentils with onyx, beans with amber, and rice with pearls—dishes it is not too hard to imagine in a high-end restaurant today.

Elagabalus was beheaded and, by the standard we apply to Rome, we are due for a comeuppance, too. The big picture about food is frightening: the Western diet overexploits unsustainable resources and, increasingly, our bad habits are being embraced by rapidly industrializing countries with large populations. In the aftermath of Michael Pollan's *The Omnivore's Dilemma,* which demonstrated the problem with a food system devoted to beefsteak and corn, Americans are opening up to previously unthinkable alternatives. In ambitious restaurants, the mainstream twentieth-century Western diet, with its narrow array of acceptable animals and plants, is being questioned. Most of what I consider here is eaten for pleasure—it is expensive, nonessential—but often it refers to necessity, the kind of deep, bone-licking eating that people do when they must milk every last calorie.

Daniel Pauly, a marine ecologist who studies global fisheries, believes that we are not so much changing our preferences as reacting to forces we choose to deny. "This idea of 'liking things' is actually a reflection of the pressure on the environment," he says. "You like what you can get. I grew up in Switzerland eating lots of horse meat because it was cheaper, and so I liked horse meat. China has had an immense population for a long time and cannot afford to be very selective. They eat anything that moves." *Anything that moves*: using that phrase about another culture's eating habits used to be an insult. Now it is a foodie-to-foodie brag, used to celebrate unchecked appetite. Taken another way, it speaks to the hidden side of food culture, where markets are created and desire is conjured; it's a seller's guiding principle. But Pauly is a scientist interested in evolutionary tactics—he admires survival—and, like the foodies who have adopted the expression as their proud credo, he means it as a compliment.

Writing this book, I set out to explore the outer bounds of food culture, where the psychological, rational, legal, ethical, and indeed physical limits of edibility are being tried— and sometimes overturned. What I found was a collection of go-betweens, chefs, and adventurous eaters—scofflaws, innovators, and crusaders—who are breaking with convention to reshape the American palate. Eating alongside them tested my stamina and tolerance for risk. There were things I was surprised to learn I could not bring myself to eat, and others I was disturbed to discover I relish. In our contemporary cuisine, I see anxiety behind the hedonism and resourcefulness tricked out as decadence. After centuries of perfecting the ritual of "civilized" dining, there is a furious backpedaling, a wilding, even among the chefs who employ the most cutting-edge techniques. At the same time, the traditional foods of poverty are being recast as elite. It is the height of sophistication to tear the meat from an animal's bones with your teeth and bare hands. To look at the food for sale in our best restaurants, you'd think that our civilization had peaked and collapsed; what we see on our plates is a post-apocalyptic free-for-all of crudity and refinement, technology and artlessness, an unimaginable future and a forgotten past.

In the past couple of years, extreme foodie-ism has become astonishingly mainstream. In December 2012, when talk of the Mayan apocalypse was in the air, Gevork Kazanchyan, a former L.A. County health inspector, hosted a multicourse dinner, with craft-beer pairings, at a barbecue restaurant in Long Beach—hardly a culinary epicenter. Advertising the event, Kazanchyan had called for only "brave, open-minded diners with no medical nor psychological restrictions on what they can consume." It was an outrageous requirement—whose diet contains *no* restrictions?—but it was only slightly more explicit in its demands than what high-end restaurants today routinely ask of their patrons. Beside each place setting was a stack of sealed envelopes containing descriptions of the courses, which were to be kept secret until after each was served—taste first, judge later.

Kazanchyan is in the unfortunate position of loving food yet knowing too much about microbiology to be at ease when eating it. Sometimes, the food-safety geek in him prevails. "It was a bunch of new-age gastro-enthusiasts versus me," he told me, describing a recent party at his house. "A buddy of mine who's a craft cocktailian and Ph.D. student in organic chem came over and was making egg-based cocktails. I was like, 'Dude, why are you not using pasteurized eggs?' He's like, 'Dude, it's one in twenty thousand.' I'm like, 'It doesn't make it a permissible safe practice.'" In November 2012, Kazanchyan published a cover story in the *Journal of Environmental Health* about the potential hazards of artisanal cocktails: fresh produce, raw eggs, and hand-shaped ice. "Unfortunately, theatrical components may not be quite so compatible with applicable public health regulations," he wrote—even though they taste "all sorts of good."

Sixty people showed up to the dinner in Long Beach. I sat down next to a guy named Thad, who was in his mid-twenties, with dark, slick-backed hair, dark jeans rolled at the cuff, argyle socks, and a leather jacket. He was from West Virginia, and he still had a bit of a twang. Across the table were his friends Erika and Kevin. The three of them had met a few years earlier, working at an Apple store deep in the San Fernando Valley. They were ordinary young aspiring professionals. I asked Thad what brought him. "The food," he said emphatically. "I'm hoping for brains. Hearts. Bone marrow."

Erika was from Bolivia, accustomed to all of those things but afraid of most seafood. She let on that she was a little nervous. "Nervous means excited," Kevin said. He was half Salvadoran and half Vietnamese, an unflappable eater. He's had eel heart, still beating, and he's pretty sure he's eaten dog, marked as "meat," in Vietnamese restaurants in L.A. With Filipino friends he tried *balut*, an unhatched duckling, cooked in its shell and eaten entire: eyes, beak, feathers, and bones. *Balut*, a Manila street food, has a reputation among American foodies for being one of the most psychologically challenging things you can eat. A blogger who writes with equanimity about eating python calls it his "culinary heart of darkness." To me, the idea was horrifying in its simplicity: an unmediated encounter with food, and with lots of parts—feathers, beak—that are decidedly *not* food. And not so much as a sprig of parsley to distract the eye.

Thad grew up eating green beans boiled to gray and burned pork chops and, when he was of age, drinking Miller Lite. After getting hooked on food porn on TV, he decided to read Anthony Bourdain, the former chef whose uninhibited approach to eating has inspired a nation of food adventurers. Thad became obsessed with finding the kinky stuff. "You can eat anything," he said. "There's so many stipulations, like 'Oooooh the texture, oooooh sweetbreads.' But if it's prepared the right way it can be great." He started eating at places where he could get pigs' ears and tails and organ meats, and he has accepted that there are certain kinds of finicky girls he can no longer date. Being in Los Angeles gives him a huge advantage. "You can find just about everything if you look," he said.

The first course came out: a Kumamoto oyster in a petri dish, in a matrix of coriander-flavored agar gel, with habanero cotton candy and several oils that, through the use of tapioca maltodextrin, had been made to resemble "a festering disease." Erika looked dubious. "No preconceptions, no fear," Thad said, digging into the awful, slippery, gummy mess.

We ate *huitlacoche*—corn fungus—alongside snails and black trumpet mushrooms. "We wanted this to be a little uncomfortable," the chef said. "*Huitlacoche* is the most famous of the gross decomposers. Farmers used to get really upset when they'd find it on their corn, until they figured out that they could sell it for three times per pound what corn costs. It's

ridiculously expensive—ours cost thirty-one dollars a pound."
Accompanying the course was a Belgian brown beer made with
deer sinews and tendons from a Chinese apothecary, and birds'
nests that the brewer stole from his mother.

"I'm waiting for the body parts," Thad said. When a course
of octopus tentacles came out, still wiggling, Kazanchyan provided instruction. "Pulverize the tissue," he said. "It needs to
stop moving before you swallow it." Otherwise, he said, the tentacles might lodge in the throat—a problem that is said to cause
several deaths a year in Korea, and makes live octopus among
the most dangerous foods in the world. "Right up there with
blowfish and rhubarb," he said. "Now we're talking," Thad said.
Everybody chewed for a long time. A sucker attached itself to
the inside of Thad's lip.

"I'm offended by the word *foodie*," Thad said at last. By this
time he was drinking my beer.

Kevin pointed at him. "*You're* a foodie," he said. "You have
a list."

"What is the definition?" Thad said, tucking into a stuffed
lamb heart. "Wanting to explore and eat anything out of the
norm? We're becoming more open. Young people are more
open. I am not a foodie, Goddamn it. I just like good food."

Jonathan, a strawberry-blond roaster at an artisanal coffee
shop in Orange County, espoused a more complex view. Late in
history, with America's institutions crumbling around them, he
and his friends felt mistrustful, even paranoid. They had retreated
into Home Ec, believing that if the worst were to happen, at
least they'd know how to pickle their own vegetables. "Our

generation feels lost," he said. "We're wanting to be self-sufficient." Near the end of the meal, Thad got his marrow. It was made into a ridiculously rich crème brûlée, which was served in a hollowed-out femur bone the chef had sawed himself.

So is foodie-ism greed or resourcefulness? If it were a matter of survival, there would be no difference. But this movement is about pleasure—pleasure heightened at the brink of calamity. Thad flashed a bright white smile and said, "If this is the end of the world, give me a fork and a knife."

PART I

SQUISHY OR SWANK?

One

THE SCAVENGER

Before I ever met Jonathan Gold, I saw him, at the far end of the bar at a pizzeria, packed tight in a black leather jacket; a cascade of graying red hair curling over his shoulders; twitchy, restless blue eyes scanning the room with the herky-jerky motion of an ink-jet printer. His broad, pale, freckled hands were crossed on the counter; the sleeves of his jacket ended a good two inches above his wrists. By then I'd been reading him in the *LA Weekly* and hearing his views on food recited like gospel among my friends for a couple of years. When, in 2007, Gold won the Pulitzer Prize for criticism, a first for a food writer and for the *Weekly,* I asked him to meet me for lunch. I was curious about the man and the food, but more than that, I was curious about the purchase that his fringy approach to eating seemed to be gaining on American cuisine. He wrote, "Let me know whether you'd rather go squishy or swank." Squishy,

I replied, and so it began, with a bowl of rubbery abalone porridge and the promise of an adventure.

Gold's dauntless approach to eating has spread to inform a new generation of American eaters. For twenty-five years, he has been chronicling the city's carts and stands and dives and holes-in-mini-malls; its Peruvian, Korean, Uzbek, Isaan Thai, and Islamic Chinese restaurants; the places that serve innards, insects, and extremities. He works the bottom of the food chain, telling his readers where to get crickets, boiled silkworm cocoons, and fried grasshoppers, of which he writes that "the mellow, pecan-like flavor isn't bad." His readers learn to appreciate the sweet rewards of the repulsive, the dangerous, the emotionally complex. "He got me into *sesos* tacos"—brains— "and *uni*, chicken feet, pig's ears, and lots of organ meat," a downtown nightlife entrepreneur told me. The only thing Gold fears is scrambled eggs; his first food memory is of pushing away a plate of them.

Selling food depends on euphemism—if we really knew what we were eating, the thinking goes, we would reject it— and often critics further empurple the industry's own florid prose. Gold is a disabuser, a champion of the real. His descriptions repel as much as they beckon; the pleasure of his prose, in the service of ghastly sounding dishes, is itself an argument that something can be awful and delightful at the same time. Sea cucumbers, he writes, "breathe through their anuses, and when attacked, some of them defend themselves by farting out sections of their poisonous, sticky lungs. The particular, ganky texture expressed by the title ingredient in bird's-nest soup is supposed to come from the fondness of the swallows in question for impaling and sucking the mucus from sea cucumbers." Writing about a Uighur restaurant in Koreatown—"a nondescript corner dining room where northeastern Chinese cooks prepare the Beijing version of Xinxiang barbecue for a Korean-speaking clientele"—he recommended what he called "the winciest dish in town: a sharp, glistening steel skewer stabbed through thin coins of meat sliced from a bull penis, which bubble and hiss when they encounter the heat of the fire, sizzling from proud quarters to wizened, chewy dimes." To him, blowfish-eating is "heightened by danger, flavored with death."

As the patron saint of foodies, Gold rightly suspects that he has encouraged what he calls the "dining as sport" crowd. "These are the guys who say, 'I'll see your live octopus and raise you a chicken foot. Oh, so you're going to eat small intestine full of undigested cow's milk?'" he said. "That's actually a good dish. You can get it at just about any taqueria, but you really have to trust the guy." One avid reader told me, "He has a lot to do with people eating at restaurants with a C from the health department. He trumpeted that really loudly, like 'I do not care! This is going to make me sick and I'm interested in endangering myself.'" Another told me that he was once laid up for two weeks after eating Korean beef-liver sashimi at a restaurant recommended by Gold. "I feel that because he's willing to eat this stuff, it's almost like a dare," he said. "I have to try it, even if it's horrifying."

Alice Waters, the chef at Chez Panisse, in Berkeley, and the mother figure of organic, farm-to-table dining, says that Gold is a harbinger of where American eating needs to go: toward diversity, away from monoculture. Gold reveals, before the U.S. Census Bureau does, which new populations have come to town, where they are, and what they're cooking up. In 2009, he announced a migration from Mexico's Distrito Federal. How did he know? Because you could now get DF-style *carnitas* in Highland Park, "loose and juicy, spilling out of the huge $1.99 tacos like Beyoncé out of a tight jumpsuit." It was the same month that the Centers for Disease Control confirmed the first two U.S. cases of swine flu, both in California, which had most people looking askance at pork. Gold looked at it sidelong, and bit. He recommended the *tacos de nana*—pig uterus— "chewy yet forgiving, pink and yet not, whorled in swoops and paisley shapes that defy Euclidean geometry."

Early in my apprenticeship, Gold took me through Historic Filipinotown. Filipino is one of the few kinds of cooking that Gold can't stand. "It's as if you took the worst of the U.S., Spanish, Asian, and Pacific Island cuisine and mixed them into one thoroughly unwholesome . . . I try, I really try," he told me once. Our destination was the Brooklyn Bagel Bakery, which was started in 1953 by immigrants from New York and is, he says, the single source of every good bagel in Los Angeles.

Looking back, I could have been hurt. Bagels? I got the sense that Gold, who is a gentleman, didn't want to scare me, at least not right away. We got four water bagels and three salt. In the car, tearing hunks from the one he had designated a roadie, he said, "You probably don't eat bagels. Too pure." It was a damning view of my potential and a barely veiled challenge. In any case, Brooklyn Bagel was only a pit stop. We had just had a so-so Guatemalan meal (*chiles relleños*, tamales, pounded-pumpkin-seed stew, and *kakik de gallina,* a chicken dish that he'd never seen on a menu before), and were on the way to Mama's Hot Tamales Café, off MacArthur Park, near Langer's Deli (the source of the city's best pastrami). "This is one of the gnarlier, gnarlier drug zones in L.A.," he said, circling Mama's block. "I was here with my mother, on our way to Langer's, and people were trying to sell her crack." An apartment where he lived for ten years, until the 1992 riots trashed the neighborhood and he moved to Pasadena, was just a couple of miles away.

At Mama's, we had a chicken tamale with red sauce and a pork tamale with green. Gold took a pound of coffee beans to go, and then we swung back west, to hit a Peruvian restaurant owned by Koreans that sits in a median, next to a car wash, and specializes in spit-roasted chicken and grilled beef heart. "It's not the *best* grilled beef heart you've ever had," he said. He was picking up a chicken for supper and, since he was there, ordered a fermented-corn drink and half a chicken to stay. I smiled weakly and said nothing. At that point, I hadn't had any grilled beef heart, ever, as I'm sure he had deduced.

Gold eats at three hundred to five hundred restaurants every year. "Food rewards obsessiveness," he says. His friend Robert Sietsema told me that, during three years starting in the late nineties, when Gold was working in New York as the restaurant critic at *Gourmet,* Sietsema, who was the restaurant critic for the *Village Voice* and presumably accustomed to eating a lot, gained twenty-five pounds. "We really put on the feed bag," he said. Not long before we talked, Sietsema said, Gold had visited. "He and I went on a typical binge. We started with porchetta sandwiches, then went to David Chang's bakery for focaccia with kimchi, then we had salty-pistachio soft-serve ice cream, cookies, and coffee milk. Then we went to a pizzeria famous for its artichoke slice, where we also had a Sicilian slice, and then we took the train to Flushing and visited a new Chinese food court and had half a dozen Chinese dishes there. Then we went to the old food court down the street, visited three more stalls, and had a bunch of things, including lamb noodles, and then Jonathan had to go to dinner somewhere. After dinner, he stopped by my apartment, and we went out to another three-course dinner." Sietsema told me, "Jonathan once said, 'We don't write about food, we write about eating.'"

When Gold took the job at *Gourmet*, maître d's around the city hastened to get a bead on his appearance. The word went out: "Biker." Wednesday was bear night in the West Village, where he lived, and he became an object of desire. "I felt like I was walking around naked," he says. Gold has been mistaken for the chef Jonathan Waxman—"another hairy Californian"—and for Mario Batali, though, according to him, "I'm much better-looking than Mario." Gold was a music journalist in the eighties and nineties. His hip-hop name, given to him by Snoop Dogg and Dr. Dre, is Nervous Cuz. He is sly and erudite, withdrawn in person and in print exuberant. The avant-garde composer Carl Stone, who has titled many of his pieces after restaurants that Gold has introduced him to, considers him the S. J. Perelman of food.

Gold grew up in South Central, the eldest of three boys. His mother, Judith, was the librarian at a rough public school, a witty, lively woman who had been a magician's assistant and a minor theater actress. His father, Irwin, an aspiring academic, studied under Joyce-scholar Richard Ellmann but got polio before he could finish his dissertation. He became a probation officer; Roman Polanski was one of his cases. The filmmakers behind the documentary *Roman Polanski: Wanted and Desired* used Irwin's copious, finely written probation report in their research. He was passionate about classical music, literature, and comfort food (Chicago-style hot dogs, all-you-can-eat buffets, lunch-counter burgers); aiming to please him, Jonathan took up cello, reading, and eating. In spite of his efforts, he failed to win his father's approval: Irwin claimed never to have read his columns. After his father died, Jonathan cleaned out Irwin's car and found a complete file of his columns in the trunk and Verdi's *Requiem* in the tape deck.

At sixteen, Gold left the house. It was the late seventies; he stayed with friends and, he says, in the months before the Iranian Revolution, squatted in Beverly Hills houses that had been bought but not yet occupied by families from Tehran. On the strength of his cello playing, he went to UCLA, where for a time he lived in his practice room. During his freshman year, Gold took a course in cultural geography and was assigned to make an ethnic map of a block of Beverly Boulevard not far from downtown. The city's variegated, unassimilated complexity began to dawn on him. At a laundromat, he saw Salvadorans saving dryers for Salvadorans, and overheard Mexicans who spoke not Spanish but Nahuatl. The 7-Eleven, he noticed, was owned by Koreans. Just as important, the block included Shibucho—one of the first Japanese restaurants, Gold says, to expel patrons for ordering California rolls—and he tried sushi. Later, for a class that he took with the performance artist Chris Burden, Gold made a piece that involved going to every Jewish deli in the city and buying two water bagels using only pennies; one he ate and one he saved to hang behind plastic on the studio wall. That was how he discovered the Brooklyn Bagel Bakery.

After graduating UCLA, Gold was living on Pico Boulevard, above a kosher butcher in an Iranian Jewish enclave, and working at a legal newspaper downtown. Taking the bus east on Pico every day, he passed through Korean, Nicaraguan, Salvadoran, Oaxacan, and Jaliscan neighborhoods. As an experiment, he set out to try every restaurant—places that served *pupusas,* chili fries, Korean barbecue—along the boulevard. He gave himself a year, at the end of which he planned to join the Foreign Service, so that he could go off and have adventures around the world. When he was finished eating Pico, he realized that he could have just as exotic a life without ever leaving Los Angeles.

For years, Gold's itinerant eating seemed purposeless; then, suddenly, as with the caterpillar in the Eric Carle book, there was a glorious, fully realized point to it. John Powers, a film critic who met Gold at the *Weekly* in the mid-eighties, when Gold was a proofreader there, says, "He has the flâneur instinct. In all those years, when his peers were very busy professionally writing, Jonathan was professionally wandering around not writing. By background, inclination, and practice, he has always been the one who knows the most stuff close to the ground." Even now, his approach can be exhausting and, to others, anticlimactic. Jervey Tervalon, a novelist who often accompanies Gold on his food tours, remembers weeks spent looking for good blood sausage soup. "The relentlessness of that search!" he said. "The leads led here and there and finally ended with a big frothy bowl of something that looked like it had a scab on top."

At the *Weekly*, when Gold was in his mid-twenties, he met Laurie Ochoa, a beautiful, dark-haired intern who had just finished college, and wooed her with dollar seats for the Los Angeles Philharmonic at the Hollywood Bowl and a slice of his mother's peach pie. They got married, over a roast pig, in 1990, and she has been his dining companion and first reader ever since. (She was his editor at *Gourmet* and at the *Weekly*.) They have two children, Leon, who is ten, and Isabel, nineteen. Isabel grew up on tentacles but can't abide anything spicy; Leon has spent his childhood ordering chicken and rice in places that specialize in blood and tripe.

The formal rigor that Gold applied to his early eating jags has become a recurring motif. He likes a culinary picaresque, and often takes the kids. They have accompanied him on hot dog, hot chocolate, and gelato sprees. The day he decided to find the city's best espresso, he traveled with David Kendrick, then the drummer for Devo. After twenty-seven shots, Gold—sweating, trembling, and talking too loudly—met up with Ochoa and some friends for dinner. He started to panic and begged the group not to get dessert. When Ochoa ordered tiramisu, he burst into tears, ran out of the restaurant, and took the bus home.

. . .

Los Angeles is an immigrant city positioned between two major foci of historical necessity eating, Latin America and Asia. This is where Gold concentrates his efforts. Interesting cuisine, he believes, often comes out of poverty. "I have my thing," he says. "Traditional—I hate the word 'ethnic'—restaurants that serve some actual hunger people have, rather than something they tell themselves they must have." Plus, there is George Orwell's rule of thumb: the fancier the restaurant, the more people who have dripped sweat into your food. For a period in the late eighties, Ochoa told me, Gold had a theory that you could tell a great restaurant based on three factors: the curtains in the window, the look of the sign, and the music that was playing (the worse, the better). One day, in Westminster, a Vietnamese enclave, he found a place with all the indicators, down to the perfectly tattered lace curtains. "We order and the waiter says, 'You don't want this dish,'" Ochoa said. "Now, we've been told that many times. We said, 'No, we really, really want it.' 'No, you don't,' he said. We said, 'We want to eat what Vietnamese people eat.' So they brought the dish out finally. It was boar, and the pieces actually had hair still on them. At this point we *had* to eat it because we'd made this whole big deal. It was pretty foul, and it wasn't just the hair."

Gold drives twenty thousand miles a year in search of food. "I go into a fugue state, like the Aboriginal dreamtime, when you go on long, aimless walks in the outback," he says. "That's how I feel driving on the endless streets of Los Angeles County." Any given afternoon will find him heading east from Pasadena into the far reaches of the San Gabriel Valley, an expansive territory of suburban cities and unincorporated towns northeast of Los Angeles whose culinary significance Gold has long asserted. "When the world's great food cities are being discussed, Paris and Tokyo and Taipei and Rome, it would not be unreasonable to include among them . . . San Gabriel, Calif., population 30,072, which up until a few years ago was noted chiefly for the patty melts at Sandi's Coffee Shop," he wrote in 1992. "Consider this: the city of San Gabriel has at least 50 restaurants worth recommending, far more than Beverly Hills or Cincinnati, and scarcely fewer than Los Angeles' entire Westside."

Over the past thirty years, the San Gabriel Valley has transformed from working-class white suburbs of faded bowling alleys and German restaurants into a place where it is possible to live quite comfortably speaking nothing but Chinese. In the seventies, Frederic Hsieh, a Chinese immigrant, successfully pitched the San Gabriel Valley city of Monterey Park to wealthy Taiwanese as "the Chinese Beverly Hills"; by 1990, according to *The Ethnic Quilt*, a book about the demographics of Southern California, the city was 36 percent Chinese and known as Little Taipei. Eating in the San Gabriel Valley, Gold has observed that, unlike in New York, where immigrants quickly adapt their cooking styles to reflect the city's collective idea of "Chinese food," the insular nature of Los Angeles allows imported regional cuisines to remain intact, traceable almost to the restaurant owners' villages of origin. "The difference is that in New York they're cooking for us," Gold told me. "Here they're cooking for themselves."

Gold's car is a green pickup: toothpicks in the cup holder,

mint-flavored Scope in the passenger's footwell. "Alice Waters gave me total shit when I bought it," he told me. "I told her, 'You know how many organic turnips I can fit in the back of this truck?' I just thought it was beautiful. It's big, and I'm big." One day, we alighted at a mini-mall in Rowland Heights, deep in the SGV. "This is the rich Chinese neighborhood," he said. From his pocket he pulled the folded-up flap of an envelope, which was covered with notes scrawled haphazardly in pencil. He wanted to try No. 1 Noodle House, where the specialty is Saliva Chicken. "So hot it makes your mouth water, which is the best of all possible reasons it might be called that," he said. He had learned about the restaurant in the Chinese-language Yellow Pages. Gold doesn't speak or read any language but English; he has strong deductive skills, and Google Translate helps. When in doubt, he points.

The noodle shop was closed. Gold consulted his notes, and we drove a hundred yards to another mini-mall. "We just did something very Californian," he said. "Drove from one shopping center across the street to another." There was a Szechuan restaurant with a string of red chilies draped over the door and a B in the window, a grade given by the county health inspector and posted by law. (Gold subscribes to another rating system, where A stands for "American Chinese," B is "Better Chinese," and C is "Chinese food for Chinese," but he admits that, for years before the grading system was in place, he walked around with constant low-level food poisoning.) He sat down and perused a menu that had been awkwardly translated into English: "Steamed Toad" was the name of one entrée. The waitress came, and he pointed to *dam–dam* noodles, dumplings, wontons, pork, and a fish special. From a cold case, he chose pig's ear. It was my first. It was oddly flavorless, but the texture reminded me of biting on a knuckle, unstable and unforgiving at once. "Some places they just slice the ear," Gold said. "Here they sliced it and pressed it into a kind of terrine, so this is probably a good place." As I chewed, my hand kept wanting to reach up and touch my own ear as a reference point.

"*Cha*, please," he said, ordering tea.

"Huh?" the waitress said.

"*Cha*—tea," he said.

"Oh, *tea*."

The fish arrived, blue-lipped and bathed in chilies and oil. "Spicy," Gold said, tasting it. "The dumplings are good, too. And I suspect they smoke their own pork here. It's good, but I don't think it's enough better than the other good Szechuan place, which is twenty miles closer to L.A." The food was heavy. "They're cooking the peasant version of these dishes," he said. "Oil is a sign of generosity."

Before heading back, Gold wanted to check out a fast food restaurant called Malan Han Noodle, in yet another mini-mall. "This place in China is the equivalent of McDonald's," he said as he approached the door. "It's the biggest chain, and it's owned by a big petroleum company. The noodles it serves are a specialty of Lanzhou, which is known for being one of the most polluted cities in China—and for its hand-pulled noodles." Inside, Gold sat down and ordered a couple of bowlfuls—large round noodles in beef broth, noodles with brown sauce. The kitchen was visible from the dining area. "Note the Mexican guy rolling out the dough and tossing the noodles," he said, tucking into his soup. "I don't know why, but that always makes me extremely happy."

In foodie mythology, Gold's traverse of Pico has the significance that Siddhartha's search for enlightenment does in Buddhism. Kate Krader, the restaurant editor of *Food & Wine,* says, "The fact that he saw the potential of every restaurant, big and small, fancy and humble, has empowered a lot of people to see the glory in the coffee that's served at their coffee shop, not to mention the person who's making the perfect grilled cheese sandwich just down the block from them." Without him, Krader says, Yelp, a site where amateurs post reviews, would not exist as we know it. For Yelpers, tweeters, bloggers, and other eating documentarians, Gold is also the one to beat.

Javier Cabral, a would-be protégé of Gold, started writing a blog called *The Teenage Glutster: Food, Adolescence, Angst, Hormones and a Really, Really Fast Metabolism* when he was sixteen and a junior in high school. (Now that he's of age, he blogs at *The Glutster.*) When I first met him, at a Vietnamese-Chinese restaurant with Corinthian columns, wedding bunting, a mural of Angkor Wat on the wall, and the whiff of cleaning fluid in the air, he was nineteen, six feet three, and weighed 135 pounds. He was wearing a purple hooded sweatshirt, a T-shirt with a picture of a pineapple on it, and thick-soled purple leopard print T.U.K.s. At the time, he was living with his parents, first-generation immigrants from Mexico, in the back room of their secondhand-furniture store in East Los Angeles.

In addition to being Cabral's "food role model," Gold was

his informant on this restaurant's unofficial Cambodian menu. From it, Cabral ordered steamed coconut fish cakes, king crab with scallions and jalapeños, and a salad made of a bitter, green, mulberry-shaped fruit. "*Sdao* is a typical herb in Cambodia," he said. "Like a broccoli texture with a super-medicinal aftertaste. It's a shame they don't have deer today, which is why I came."

In his early teens, Cabral told me, he was "non-food-conscious," eating fast food all the time. When he learned about PETA, he became a vegan. "I started to get brainwashed," he said. "But that was my gateway, and it led me to get more interested in food." The real transformation came when, in an act of self-preservation—to get away from the temptations of East L.A.: punk rock and beer—he decided to move in with his sister in Alhambra, in the San Gabriel Valley, so he could attend "a high-achieving Asian-driven school." He picked up an *LA Weekly* looking for information about punk shows, and noticed that many of the restaurants being reviewed were within walking distance of his school. While his classmates went in packs to In-N-Out, he'd go alone for Szechuan takeout, which he'd eat in the back alley. "I learned from Jonathan Gold that food writing doesn't need to be so hosh-posh, snobby, and froufrou," the Glutster told me. "It can be ghetto." So he started his own blog. "At first, I was the only food blogger in L.A. with no pictures, because I couldn't afford a camera."

Several years ago, the Glutster's mother took him to a healing mass at La Iglesia Nuestra Señora de la Soledad, his local parish, in the hope that it would cure him of his fascination with food, which she finds worrisome. He left before the service ended, and, taking a walk around the neighborhood, came upon the day's true "revelation," as he put it on his blog: a Oaxacan spot, Moles La Tia, that served twenty varieties of mole. Later, Gold reviewed the restaurant and credited the Glutster with the find, thereby putting him on the food-blogging map.

Over lunch, Cabral told me it had been five years since he ate fast food. With Gold's guidance, he has explored delicacies from the neighborhood where he grew up—goat stew and tongue tacos—which he'd never tried before. He eats his way through any food festival he can score tickets to. At one, he ran into his mentor after trying food from every vendor and sometimes going back for seconds. "So, Mr. Gold, how do you deal with this nasty, disgusting feeling of repulsement?" he asked. "Ach, you'll get used to it," was the answer. Cabral's solution was to walk the five miles home to East L.A.

Not long after his discovery of Moles La Tia, Cabral found out about a place called Pal Cabron, which was serving street food from Puebla, the state just north of Oaxaca. In a post that reflected something of Gold's penchant for the earthily figurative, he rhapsodically chronicled the "Avocado, Chipotle, and the ever acquired taste of Papalo, an herb that smells like if a really thirsty deer just walked on top of it." In other words, it tasted of deer pee, and that was a good thing. This time, when Gold wrote up the restaurant, a week later, he didn't cite the Glutster's review. Cabral tweeted in protest—"J. Gold . . . give me credit!"—to no avail.

Pal Cabron, which has since closed, was in the heavily Mexican neighborhood of Huntington Park. Bricia Lopez, whose parents opened Guelaguetza, the city's first Oaxacan restaurant, is a glamorous young fixture of the L.A. food scene. She started Pal Cabron with her brother. They decorated the inside of the restaurant with bright colors and murals of dishy women, each embodying a different saucily named sandwich from her menu: La Tuya (Yo Momma), La Tetanic (The Double-D), La Muy Muy. The doorway was painted with the screen icons of Facebook, Twitter, and Yelp. The place, according to its décor, was a product of foodie social media; survival, in this off-the-beaten-path location, would depend on Gold's pilgrims.

After we had gorged on Cambodian food, the Glutster suggested we make a trip to Pal Cabron, to get his favorite *cemita*, a sandwich of seasoned lamb and *quesillo*, served on a crunchy, house-made sesame roll. He was emboldened by his recent reviewing triumphs. "Gold used to be my role model. Now he's—dare I say it?—my competition," he mused. "A role model–slash–supercelebrity–slash–archenemy." Cabral has many times offered himself up to Gold as an assistant; he wants to help him put together a long-promised follow-up to *Counter Intelligence*, a compendium of reviews Gold published more than a decade ago. But Gold has been elusive. "Probably he's scared because he knows I'm going to dethrone him one day," Cabral speculated. He walked through the restaurant and chose a table facing the back wall. There, Bricia had commissioned another mural, this one depicting Jonathan Gold, eyes cast down and smiling over a little double chin, next to his *LA Weekly* review. His arm was outstretched, with one hand gently touching the Glutster's computer screen.

To Gold's readers, his reviews have the ontological status that *The New York Times* has for people who follow the news: he doesn't write about it because it is; it is because he's written about it. In the spring of 2009, he published a column titled "The New Cocktailians," about the movement of dandified bartenders who pair suspenders with tattoos and treat drinks as a culinary art, shopping at farmers' markets for fresh produce and educating customers about the origins of the gin fizz. By fall, all food-minded Los Angeles understood, without knowing exactly how or why it knew, that a cocktail moment was in full swing.

Then Gold hosted a benefit event at Union Station, the train depot downtown. There were concoctions from New Cocktailians (Manhattans made with Luxardo cherries, champagne drinks with absinthe-citrus foam), paired with morsels from some of Gold's favorite highbrow places. Gold, wearing a gray suit and a pale pink tie covered in pink velvet polka dots, stood with Ochoa at a cocktail table. "The chefs are going to freak out if you don't eat anything," she said, and went to get him a plate.

Ochoa came back with a pig slider and a pig's ear, a deep-fried, molten triangle, uncomfortably soft. "I definitely encourage a certain kind of cooking," Gold said, popping the ear and then the slider into his mouth. Then he went to search for bacon-wrapped matzoh balls: the ultimate transgression.

The food nerds were out in force: bloggers from the local sites that track Gold's every move. Neil Kohan—thirty-one, receding hair, camera slung over his shoulder—sipped a Manhattan and declared Gold the Thom Yorke of food writing. (His blog, *Food Marathon*, chronicles his eating itineraries, many of them heavily informed by Gold.) Another blogger urged Gold to try her drink—twelve-year-old Scotch, ginger syrup, fresh lime juice, soda water, and crushed ice, also made from Scotch. He sipped. "It's delicious," he said. "But something about it tastes a little like pool water, too."

Following in Gold's footsteps can be hazardous. For many years, at the *Weekly*, Gold produced an annual list called "99 Essential L.A. Restaurants." Ken Baumann, an actor, attempted to eat at every one, but ended up having part of his colon and small intestine removed—Crohn's disease—after ticking off only twenty-eight. Gold's last list for the *Weekly* came out in the fall of 2011. Jenji Kohan, the creator of *Weeds*, and her husband, Christopher Noxon, a writer, decided to tackle it. They are committed eaters and devotees of Gold, and they felt they needed some way to structure their dining. "If you have a curator and you have a project that allows you to focus down, it gives you clarity," Noxon says.

By June, Kohan and Noxon were on their sixtieth of the "99": Lukshon, an upscale restaurant owned by Sang Yoon, the chef Gold credits with starting the national plague of "Changes and Modifications Politely Declined" when he added that language to the menu at his burger place, Father's Office. I met them there for dinner.

"Jonathan Gold says we have to get the squid, and we listen to Jonathan Gold over all things," Kohan said as we sat down. She had on a red cardigan and cat's-eye glasses. Noxon, thin and fair, added tea-leaf salad, Manila clams, Chinese black mushrooms, garlic pork belly. The waiter suggested lamb belly roti; we got two. "He's got a tender tummy, which was a problem initially," Kohan said. "I have an iron stomach. My mother cooked like a cafeteria—mediocre food and a *lot* of it."

"At a certain point, I would have taken a pill for daily caloric intake," Noxon said. "Now I get angry if I have something that isn't delicious. I get depressed."

Once they both cared, choosing where to eat grew complicated. "It was hugely contentious and difficult," Noxon said. "An unbelievable ordeal. Where are we going to eat? What continent?" Sometimes they would spin the globe to settle it. Now they have three children, who bicker in the car on Saturday mornings about whether to go to Golden Deli, a Vietnamese spot in San Gabriel that is perennially on the "99," or to La Cabañita, in the far-flung town of Montrose, for Mexican. Charlie, the eldest, is thirteen. "He is the most adventurous, and the most limited," Kohan said—allergic to dairy, sesame, and cashews. A few years ago, he decided to keep kosher, though his parents aren't observant, and now he avoids pork and shellfish, except on Purim. "He found a loophole in the literature that says on Purim you are 'not yourself,' so for one day a year it's blue crab hand rolls and pork soup dumplings, the things he misses."

At the end of dinner, Noxon said, "Those mushrooms are amazing and I will crave them." They were meaty and deep, with a touch of smoke, like the dregs of a pot of Lapsang souchong. They agreed that the food was tasty, but that it was the kind of place that years of reading Jonathan Gold had taught them to deplore: inauthentic, impersonal, what he calls an "AmEx restaurant." "It's really good, but it's bullshit," Noxon said. "Third generation."

I n a fancy restaurant, Gold will wear a rumpled suit and a soft bluish button-down and pay with a credit card issued in the name of his high-school algebra teacher. He has special cell phone numbers that he uses just for reservations. "It's like *The Bourne Identity* in slow motion," he says.

The first piece he wrote for a "slick"—the now defunct *California* magazine, edited by the late Harold Hayes—was a review of Chasen's, which had been an entertainment-industry staple for fifty years. To Gold, it reeked of Reaganomics and other things that he despised. He wrote that it was "a swell place to celebrate a seventy-fifth birthday or a contra incursion," and that the famous chili was "distinguishable from a bowl of Dennison's only by a couple of chunks of sirloin, a 1,600 percent price differential and three guys"—the servers—"who look like they stepped out of a 1935 gangster B-movie." He has his regrets. "Although I didn't do Chasen's in"—it was around for another decade—"I certainly put a lance in its side," he says. "But, looking back, I really miss Chasen's. And kiwi vinaigrette and magical caviar snakes and braised cantaloupe with black corn fungus and all the things I thought were the future back then—a lot of that food was just silly."

Accessible food has always been of greater interest to Gold—but it depends on what you mean by accessible. "The democracy of really fine dining is something I've always liked about L.A.," he says. "In New York, the most expensive restaurant is always the best. That's not necessarily the case here." In 1990, he started writing about Renu Nakorn, an Isaan Thai place twenty miles southeast of downtown, next to a working dairy farm. After his reviews, large numbers of white people started coming in. They ordered what he had ordered: slimy bamboo salads, fermented fish, and intensely spicy dishes—authentic regional Thai food that the owners, Bill and Saipin Chutima, were worried the customers would send back. Jeffrey Steingarten, the food critic for *Vogue*, made a pilgrimage (the Chutimas said that his postprandial cigar was disrupted by the stench of cows), and so did Mark Bittman, of *The New York Times*. When the Chutimas moved to Las Vegas and opened a new place, Lotus of Siam, Gold called it the best Thai restaurant in North America; in 2011, Saipin, who does the cooking, won a James Beard award. Gold, who has a competitive streak, put it this way once: "As the Italians say of Christopher Columbus, when he discovered America, it stayed discovered."

As a kid, Gold guzzled hot sauce. Several years ago, on a tip from a diner who had discovered a secret, untranslated menu of southern Thai specialties at an ordinary strip-mall Thai place called Jitlada, Gold paid a visit. After eating there a few times, he brought his friend Carl Stone, the composer, who carries a card in his wallet that says, more or less, in Thai, "Yes, I know I'm not Thai, but please give me the food as spicy as I request." They ordered *kua kling*, a dry-beef curry, and asked for it "Bangkok hot."

The *kua kling* was the spiciest Gold had ever had. "It was glowing, practically incandescent," he told me. "You bite into it and every alarm in your body goes off at once. It's an overload on your pain receptors, and then the flavors just come through. It's not that the hotness overwhelms the dish, which is what people who don't understand Thai cooking always say, but that the dish is revealed for the first time—its flavor—as you taste details of fruit and turmeric and spices that you didn't taste when it was merely extremely hot. It's like a hallucination. You're floating in some high, tasting the most magnificent things you've ever tasted in your life. I've never been able to get them to make it that hot again." Stone said it hurt to pee for three days afterward. He said, "I thought, How in the world could I have gotten the clap?"

That day, the owner, a voluble woman named Jazz, came over to their table and started chatting. She mentioned that she had been praying every day in her Buddha room for Jonathan Gold to come in and review her restaurant. Did they know him or know what he looked like? she asked. Stone says, "I was going to throw out a red herring—'He's tall and thin with a full head of hair'—but Jonathan started laughing and introduced himself." Gold, in his review, praised the "delicious, foul-smelling yellow curries" and the "strange, mephitic fragrances" of wild tea leaves and stinky beans, and said that Jitlada was "the most exciting new Thai restaurant of the year."

Mark Gold, the youngest of the Gold sons, runs the marine conservation organization Heal the Bay; he finds Jonathan's eating habits atrocious and enumerates his brother's gustatory offenses on his blog, *Spouting Off.* "I have gone to dim sum in San Gabriel when he tried to order shark fin soup," Mark wrote. "I said OMDB! I went to a restaurant with him in Chicago when he was the lead grub guy at *Gourmet* magazine. There, he nearly ordered wild-caught sturgeon until I complained vociferously."

Right before I met him, Jonathan made his first trip to Seoul. When he got back, he wrote about eating live octopus, or *sam nak ji*, which he described as "one of the most alarming dishes in the world." After the piece came out, Mark told me, "Needless to say, I did not participate in that sadistic torture of a wonderful marine animal. I'm not going to eat live shrimp. I'm not going to eat octopus. I haven't had shark or swordfish in twenty-five years. I said to him, 'What do you think an octopus is? You need an ecology class.' He's all, 'It doesn't have a backbone.'"

Of course, Gold didn't need to go to Korea to eat live octopus. One night he took me to a divey strip-mall restaurant with a picture of a smiling mermaid and a halibut on the sign, and a Korean golf show playing on the television set. He had guessed based on the halibut that they'd have live shrimp and *sam nak ji*. "If you're going to have live halibut you'll have *sam nak ji*," he said. "It's like ham and eggs." It turned out they were out of shrimp—the next shipment was coming at eleven o'clock that night, flown in fresh from Korea—but they had the octopus. "How do I put this delicately?" he said as we sat down. "It's a very male food. We're going to get a lot of winks and nods."

Gold said he thought that the space had once been occupied by Alex Donut, one of three places in town to get Thai food in the late seventies. "I probably wouldn't think it was good now, but that was a thousand Thai meals ago," he said. "I thought it was amusing to eat all the little green nachos in a jar of vinegar, too."

Korean sashimi came to the table—big hunks of white tuna, with the taste and texture of chilled butter; fresh-killed halibut—along with pickled mackerel eggs and sea squirts. The squirts glistened orange and tasted of brine. "These things are essentially taking over the fricking sea," Gold said. "The taste is strong, iodine-y, but not unpleasant—but some people are totally grossed out by them." The bluefin on the table went untouched. "It's the equivalent of going on the Serengeti and eating the lion," Gold said. "My brother hates this argument, but I don't like it because it's boring. Things that are at the top of the food chain are boring. They all taste the same."

Then the proprietor, suppressing a smile, produced the main event, a plate of slippery gray tentacles, squirming anxiously. "It'll try to climb up the chopstick," Gold said, dousing a tentacle in sesame oil to loosen the grip of its suckers. "I don't actually know that much about octopus physiology. Most people say that the octopus is dead, and just twitching, but I don't know. It looks pretty alive to me."

Gold bit into the octopus. "I thought I was completely full from lunch, but this is invigorating food," he said. More courses came—broiled eel and broths and a greasy red kimchi pancake and, finally, crab claws covered in a sticky glaze, lustrous as a ceramic sculpture by Jeff Koons.

He was a tad disappointed about missing the unsettling experience of eating live shrimp. "It freaks me out," he told me.

"You're picking up an animal whose carapace has been stripped off by the chef. Its eyeballs are going back and forth on its eye-sticks and it's madly trying to swim away. Prawns don't have a great deal of intelligence but they know when they're going to die. You're killing something with your teeth, and whatever the pleasure of that—and the flavor, I've got to admit, is incredibly, hedonistically sweet—it feels wrong. You're not supposed to kill things with your teeth."

Two

GRUB

The roots of extreme foodie-ism extend back to the beginning of the American gourmet industry, when squishy and swank were often one and the same. The business, which, in 2012, represented 10 percent of retail food sales and was worth nearly $86 billion, was built by a handful of largely forgotten European refugees on the backs of a menagerie of creatures most people in this country would gag to see on a plate of food.

At first, the specialty-food trade was based on comforting people with the familiar. During World War II, as thousands of Jews fled Europe for the United States, Jewish importers, most of them working from offices on Hudson and Varick Streets in lower Manhattan, supplied other émigrés with items from home. Only when the salesmen began to penetrate the uptown carriage-trade shops and department stores newly devoting floor space to imported food in spiffy packaging, did the stuff become known as "specialty." Mario Foah, who arrived from Naples in 1939, at the age of eighteen, got his start peddling panettone, a product from the north of Italy that was exotic to the southern Italians he was trying to sell to. Later, he diversified to cookies and candy. "It was strictly a Christmas business," Foah, who is ninety-three, told me. "The rest of the year we managed by starving and eating samples from our suppliers." Business was conducted in cash; according to one old story I heard, dealers kept their money in secret compartments in their shoes.

Storytelling and salesmanship were inseparable, and an aura of personal sophistication proved useful. Ted Koryn was the quintessential New York food pitchman: small and suave, hilariously funny, fluent in four languages and conversant in a handful of others. He was born in Amsterdam to a wealthy family; only French was spoken in his grandmother's dining room, and when his mother went out at night a maid had to stay up till she returned to help her undress. Left alone there during the war—his mother and stepfather had gone "on holiday" to the United States just before the Nazis invaded—he hid out on a boat with two friends, and slept in the boathouse at night. In 1942, his stepfather's uncle was able to trade his art collection for exit visas, and Koryn rejoined his family in New York. There he signed on to a Dutch attachment to the Air Force and was trained in aerial photography at Yale.

After the war, Koryn started a food business, selling mainly French products no one had ever heard of before, like Pommery mustard, Lu Biscuits, and Evian water (which never took off for him). His first wife, Miriam Metzger, was the daughter of Joe

Metzger, who co-founded Dannon yogurt in the Bronx. (The company, which began as Danone in Spain and got its original yogurt cultures from the Pasteur Institute, struggled to connect with U.S. consumers until Miriam's brother, Juan, suggested putting fruit in the bottom of the cup.) Koryn rode around Manhattan in a chauffeured limousine, and socialized constantly with an eclectic group of friends, from the cartoonist Will Eisner to the truffle-selling Urbanis and Xaviera Hollander, a former call girl who wrote *The Happy Hooker*. If he wanted someone to play poker with, he sent the car.

Koryn traveled extensively throughout Europe, always shopping for products to import. It was a good time to get deals: European manufacturers, their domestic economies destroyed, were willing to front product for the chance to enter a potentially vast American market. Purveyors played the edges. "If it was illegal or not one hundred percent, even the better," Tim Metzger, Koryn's nephew, told me. "They loved to press the rules." Bob Lape, a food journalist who started "The Eyewitness Gourmet" segment on WABC-TV in 1970, met Koryn in the middle of a blizzard, when he persuaded him to come visit his factory. Koryn was one of two men Lape called "the hungry ones." The other was Murray Klein, the legendary manager and part owner of the New York specialty store Zabar's, where Koryn sold white truffles and beluga caviar.

In the 1950s, opening a can of mushroom soup and pouring it over a casserole was a culinary event. "They were putting crap in Jell-O and calling it an aspic," John Roberts, a veteran of the food business, says. "Change was not valued. Food was not an adventure." Mario Foah told me, "If you said to the man on the street, 'I'd like to introduce you to gourmet foods,' he'd say, 'Spell it!'" In 1952, Foah, Koryn, and several others decided to form a monthly lunch club that could function as a trade association, lobbying in Washington against tariffs on European products and other issues affecting them. They called themselves the National Association for the Specialty Food Trade, or NASFT.

In 1955, the association put on its first event, the National Fancy Food and Confection Show, at the Sheraton-Astor Hotel in Manhattan. The war had sent a generation of Americans abroad, and the idea was to re-create foreign eating experiences: French mustard, Swiss chocolates, German sausages. The association's president put a note in the brochure, celebrating the inauguration of a marketplace for novel foodstuffs. "This being our first effort, there may be much to criticize and we beg your indulgence for any shortcomings or omissions," he wrote.

One of the omitted would not indulge the oversight. Max Ries, a savvy Chicago-based purveyor, who had been barred from exhibiting—he posed a threat, most likely—ran a limousine from the Sheraton-Astor to another hotel nearby, where he had set up a show of only his products. After a few years, the New Yorkers relented and gave him a booth, which became a major attraction. To his first show, Ries brought an aerosol can filled with liquid cheese spread and a gift basket that cost $300, about $2,500 today. It included a barrel-based table, four chairs, and sixty imported delicacies. Ries came away with sixty-five orders. The next year, he displayed a brightly painted Sicilian cart with an umbrella, loaded with treats. Beautiful models passed out samples. "A lot of people didn't like him," Foah told me. "But I admired him. He made people talk about the industry."

A few months after Ries's show debut, *Fortune* named his company the country's largest importer, estimating its business at $6,500,000 a year, and overall specialty-food sales as high as $200 million, double what they had been in the show's first year. Commercial jetliners were making international travel, and therefore international eating, increasingly accessible. Suburbanites had money, time, and space to entertain; they needed something provocative and delicious to impress their guests at cocktail parties. Curiosity and snobbism, the piece concluded, were leading the way to "a greater sophistication of American taste." The *Los Angeles Times* reported on a "gourmet cult which reaches now from lavish Park Avenue apartments to the grassroots split-level homes of the Middle West." The country was in the midst of a "great delicacy boom."

Ries, an outsider and a self-reinventor, helped create a taste for the freaky in a society devoted to beefsteak, glamorizing the seemingly repulsive and making it into a symbol of elegance. After a lucrative career as a textile manufacturer in Germany, he arrived in Chicago in 1939 and started selling imported European cheeses out of the back of a station wagon on Route 41, store by store. Soon he employed a brigade of German-Jewish refugees to go on the road for him. They drove all day and for dinner ate canned peaches and ice cream. Within a few years, Ries had diversified: an early price list shows Norwegian goat cheese, Bahamian mustard, chow mein noodles, Cuban rock lobster, and Hawaiian Punch.

Ries was dashing; slim and refined, he wore handmade

suits and twirled—never chewed—his cigars. In order to make his company sound more "American," he called it Reese Finer Foods. He developed new foods—baby corn, blue-cheese salad dressing, shelf-stable croutons—and sold them alongside other then-exotic fare like water chestnuts. When a shipment of artichokes arrived in rusty, dented cans, Ries packed them in glass with vinaigrette, and called them marinated artichokes. He couldn't boil water, according to his son, but he had a flair for presentation. Reese Finer Foods helped introduce teriyaki sauce to the United States by attaching a Japanese yen coin to every bottle sold ("Gives you a yen for Oriental food"); their barbecue sauce came with a whisk attached. In 1958, the *Los Angeles Evening Herald Express* announced, "Something wonderful has happened and no longer do you need ever again to get garlic on your finger tips!" Reese had invented roll-on garlic oil.

While other importers looked mainly to Europe, Ries sought unfamiliar snacks in Asia and Latin America. He brought tinned sparrows and French-fried grasshoppers from Japan, and ants from Bogotá. The Illinois candy-maker he hired to cover the ants with chocolate is said to have called Ries in a panic when the 500-pound shipment arrived; workers were threatening to quit the line. Once a year, Ries and his employees went to Asia to look for products and ideas. Reese sold tinned lion, tiger, elephant, and whale; pickled rooster combs, espresso, Lindt chocolate; Canadian muskrat, reindeer steaks from Lapland, and diamondbacks from Ross Allen, a snake-wrestling celebrity herpetologist with a ranch in Florida.

Ancient Romans sold the meat of exotic, imported panthers, hippos, lions, and giraffes killed in death matches at the

circus; Reese did the modern equivalent, tinning creatures cul-
led from zoos. "The zoos would furnish lists of animals they
had to dispose of," an employee later told a newspaper reporter.
"Reese would buy a carcass at a high price and give it, frozen, to
a cannery for processing." When Ries went to a stock show in
Chicago and noticed that no one was bidding on the bison—not
then considered food—he bought the whole lot for forty cents a
pound, and canned the meat with wine. "He took great food
that nobody knew they wanted and got them to buy it," Stewart
Reich, Ries's great-nephew, told me. "Max—I don't want to say
he churned it out, but he had a supply line and discovered the
soft part of the market and exploited it." At a "Fashion Show of
Foods" Ries put on in Milwaukee in the mid-fifties, he said,
"Eating habits are in the mind."

As early as 1965, Ries predicted the foodie movement, and
its turn toward the more inclusive, inventive cuisines of Latin
America and Asia. "More people today can afford more of the
so-called 'exotic' foods which previously were available only to
persons of great wealth," he said. "With this increased affluence
has also come a new spirit of adventure about eating." His evidence that the babyish palate of America was maturing was that
people had begun to take their baked potatoes with sour cream
instead of sweet butter.

"They were Marco Polo type of guys," Reich says. "They were
definitely in the entertainment business." One year Reese had
overstock of its Spooky Foods gift set—chocolate-covered ants,
bees, grasshoppers, and caterpillars—so it hired Bela Lugosi to
appear in his Dracula costume with the product, which promptly
sold out. Alienation was part of the appeal. Reich, who still works

in the food business, considered Ries a mentor and an example; the month that *Jaws* opened in theaters Reich hawked shark-meat pâté wearing a scuba suit and took out an advertisement that read, "This is your chance to bite back."

One of Ries's most valued employees was Morris Kushner, a former writer on Groucho Marx's *This Is Your Life*, who started as a West Coast representative and rose to company president. He lived in the guest quarters of a sprawling mansion in Encino and was married to Naudjia de Morozova, a thin, flamboyant woman who dressed in fur, claimed to be a Russian countess, and ate little besides chocolate. Kushner, who wore checked suits, a tweed trilby, and a moustache, was from Nebraska. His pedigree in food was long: his uncle was a grocer in Lincoln, and Kushner apprenticed with him in his youth. After the war, he worked for a wholesaler in Los Angeles that supplied Hollywood with chutney, caviar, and foie gras. In a book on the industry, he boasted of having been one of the first to bring smoked oysters from Japan to the United States, as part of General MacArthur's plan to revive the Japanese economy by appealing to American hostesses.

"I set out to design our private label and felt that I needed something other than merely the words 'Smoked Oysters,'" Kushner wrote. The one other similar product available at the time was a crabapple smoked oyster from the Pacific Northwest. "I searched through Japanese literature and history books. . . . From *Madame Butterfly* and the Cherry Blossom Festival, I assumed that Japan had an abundance of cherry trees, so I labeled our product 'Cherrywood Smoked Oysters.'" When he later met with the president of the Smoked Oyster Association in Hiroshima, he learned that the Japanese had been flummoxed by his first order, and had gone out in search of precious cherrywood to authenticate the label's claim. "Needless to say, that was the only time cherrywood was ever used in that manner, and subsequent orders were smoked with the cheaper kindling scrap wood." But, he concluded proudly, "cherrywood smoked" became the industry standard. "I relate this little tale to illustrate how a product can be upgraded in the eyes of the beholder with a little label imagery."

The successful food seller was part carnival barker, part con man. If an item wasn't moving, Kushner's advice was to mark it up: a $75 jar of truffles is more intriguing than the same jar for $45. Another rule of thumb: "The food broker must never lie to a buyer, or better yet, never get caught lying." In the mid-forties, when most specialty-foods dealers were trying to keep their products *out* of supermarkets for fear that mass marketing and availability would destroy their mystique (and their profit margins), he persuaded a Southern California grocery store to designate a gourmet section. They called the improvised area—a plywood shelf resting on large, foil-wrapped juice cans—"the importation center," because most of the items came from abroad. By 1970, the Safeway in Washington, D.C., stocked nearly five thousand gourmet items, among them staples of the Reese line like rattlesnake, kangaroo, and Bengal tiger meat. They may not have been a large part of the business, but they served a purpose: "shelf-warmers" tended to start selling faster when placed near such attention-grabbing exotics.

In 1968, Craig Claiborne, the food editor of *The New York Times*, wrote with amusement about Reese's elephant meat, which "the foremost food authority in Florida" was planning to serve in an omelet at her husband's restaurant in Miami. (Her source: Bloomie's.) The following year, the federal Endangered Species Conservation Act was passed, significantly expanding the prohibitions against selling certain animals, and Reese's swashbuckling period came to an abrupt end. In 1973, Congress signed the Endangered Species Act, a broader law that is still in place. That year, after tins of Reese's smoked whale meat were discovered for sale in the Gourmet Foods Shop at Macy's in New York, investigators confiscated a large supply from a Reese warehouse in the Bronx, fined the company, and made it promise not to sell any more endangered species in the state.

As the market changed, Kushner tried to live down his association with the "gimmicky" foods that had set Reese apart from its competitors. Kushner saw food both as a mark of status and as a democratizer, a powerful social vehicle for the eighties striver. "Tonight you can eat as well as Rockefeller," he'd say. In 1982, he told *The New York Times,* "When people can't afford mink coats, Cadillacs, or beautiful homes, they reward themselves with good cheeses they can afford. It's accessible luxury." By then, specialty foods had moved out of the "gourmet ghetto" and onto the supermarket's main shelves—the Grey Poupon alongside the ballpark mustard—and America had changed because of it. There were limits—Kushner didn't think *balut* would ever "go down"—but people had accepted previously spurned exotics like raw oysters, rabbit, and mussels. Kushner took to greeting visitors to the food show by saying, "Welcome to Wonderland, where today's specialties become tomorrow's staples!"

. . .

In overcoming the resistance to certain foods, Frederick J. Simoons, the author of the classic text on culinary taboos *Eat Not This Flesh*, says timing is everything, and there is usually more than one factor at play. When Emperor Meiji ate beef—a sacrilege in Buddhist Japan—it was because the country was ready to embrace the West. Noritoshi Kanai, the eighty-eight-year-old president of Mutual Trading Company, which imports gold flakes and matsutake essence to sell to high-end sushi restaurants like Masa and Nobu, introduced sushi to the United States in the 1960s. Because sushi is raw and handled without gloves in front of the customer, everyone told him that the American public would never accept it. The convergence of three factors, he says, changed their minds: the food pyramid, which emphasized fish; the rise of the Japanese car; and *Shōgun*, the best-selling novel by James Clavell.

Insects, the wiggly, bridge-party shockers that helped get America excited about eating, are back, and this time around they may, like Evian, be here to stay. The conditions are promising. America's food intelligentsia bemoans the industrial-scale farming and food processing of the present, and forsees a *Mad Max* future. Insects are danger-tinged but eco-friendly, and little explored as food. Once a staple on *Fear Factor*, they were featured on *Top Chef Masters* a few seasons ago; the winning dish was tempura-fried crickets with sunchoke-carrot purée and blood-orange vinaigrette. During the London Olympics, the celebrated Danish chef René Redzepi, whose restaurant, Noma, has repeatedly been named the best restaurant in the world, served a tasting menu at Claridge's, the five-star Mayfair hotel. The eight-course meal cost more than $300 a head and featured chilled live ants, flown from Copenhagen, on cabbage with crème fraiche. "When you bite into the ants, they release the flavor of lemongrass; what you taste is light and citrusy, in contrast to the edible soil you have just consumed," the *Bloomberg* food critic wrote.

Guelaguetza, the Oaxacan restaurant opened by Bricia Lopez's parents, serves a scrumptious plate of *chapulines a la Mexicana*—grasshoppers sautéed with onions, jalapeños, and tomatoes, and topped with avocado and Oaxacan string cheese. Lopez says that more and more Anglo hipsters—Jonathan Gold readers—are coming in to order them. "Eating grasshoppers is a thing you do here," she said. "Like, 'Oh my God, I ate a grasshopper, *woo*.'" She went on, "There's more of a cool factor involved. It's not just 'Let's go get a burrito.' It's 'Let's get a mole' or 'Let's get a grasshopper.'" According to the FDA, insects sold as human food must be raised specifically for the purpose in a facility that follows "good manufacturing processes"; "wild-crafting" is not condoned, for fear of pesticide contamination or disease, nor is diverting bugs from the pet-food stream. The USDA, which typically handles meat, doesn't contemplate insects at all. Until a citation from the health department prompted them to set up a certified facility in Oaxaca, the Lopezes got the *chapulines* they served at Guelaguetza from friends and relatives, who packed them in their carry-ons when they visited from Mexico.

The contemporary vogue for bugs reflects not only a desire

for novelty but also a degree of pragmatism, and that may guarantee their staying power. José Andrés, a winner of the James Beard Foundation's Outstanding Chef award, makes a very popular *chapulín* taco—sautéed shallots, deglazed in tequila; chipotle paste; and Oaxacan grasshoppers, in a handmade tortilla—at his Washington, D.C., restaurant Oyamel. He sees bug-eating as both a gastronomic experience (he recommends the mouthfeel of a small, young, crispy *chapulín*) and a matter of survival. "We need to feed humanity in a sustainable way," he says. "Those who know how to produce protein will have an edge over everyone else. World War Three will be over control of water and food, and the insects may be an answer."

According to the ecologist Daniel Pauly, Mexico's tradition of insect-eating arose from a lack of alternatives. Before the arrival of the Europeans, there were neither cows nor horses nor other large mammals that could be easily domesticated. The same went for the rest of Latin America: this is why Peruvians, and tourists to Cuzco, eat guinea pigs. "Even the Aztec killing machine was not able to reduce the population sufficiently," he says. "That Mexico developed a taste for bugs may be related to population pressure." He went on, "Why are we even contemplating eating insects? Because we are gradually running out of things to eat."

Demographers have projected that by 2050 the world's population will have increased to nine billion, and the demand for meat will grow with it, particularly in dense, industrializing countries like China and India. In 2010—a year in which, according to the United Nations, nearly a billion people suffered from chronic hunger—the journal *Science* published a special issue on food security, and included a piece on entomophagy, the unappealing name by which insect-eating properly goes. Acknowledging that the notion might be "unappetizing to many," the editors wrote, "The quest for food security may require us all to reconsider our eating habits, particularly in view of the energy consumption and environmental costs that sustain those habits."

From an ecological perspective, insects have a lot to recommend them. They are renowned for their small "foodprint"; being cold-blooded, they are about four times as efficient at converting feed to meat as are cattle, which waste energy keeping themselves warm. Ounce for ounce, many have the same amount of protein as beef—fried grasshoppers have three times as much—and are rich in micronutrients like iron and zinc. Genetically, they are so distant from humans that there is little likelihood of diseases jumping species, as swine flu did. They are natural recyclers, capable of eating old cardboard, manure, and by-products from food manufacturing. And insect husbandry offers an alternative to the problem of factory farming: bugs *like* teeming, and thrive in filthy, crowded conditions.

In late 2010, a group of scientists at Wageningen University, in the Netherlands, published a paper concluding that insects reared for human consumption produce significantly lower quantities of greenhouse gases than do cattle and pigs. "This study therefore indicates that insects could serve as a more environmentally friendly alternative for the production of animal protein," the paper said. One of its authors was Arnold van Huis, an entomologist who is working to establish a market for insect-based products in the Netherlands, with funding from the Dutch government; the agriculture ministry recently gave him a million euros to research insect husbandry. "We have a food crisis, especially a meat crisis, and people are starting to realize that we need alternatives, and insects are just an excellent alternative," van Huis said.

On a trip to Africa, in 1995, when van Huis was on sabbatical, he traveled to a dozen countries, interviewing locals about their relationship with insects. Half the people he spoke with talked about eating them, and he finally overcame their reluctance— born of centuries of colonial opprobrium—to share some with him. "I had termites, which were roasted, and they were excellent," he said. When he got home, he offered a bag of termites to Marcel Dicke, the head of his department. Dicke liked them, and the two men started a popular lecture series that addressed insects' potential as a food source. After van Huis and Dicke organized an insect festival that drew twenty thousand people, they were approached by several mealworm and cricket farmers who had been serving the pet-food industry but were interested in diversifying. "We know that Western peoples have some difficulties psychologically with ingesting insects, so we are looking at some ways of introducing them into food so that people will no longer recognize them," van Huis said. Insect flour was one option. "Another possibility is that you can grind insects and make them into a hot dog or a fish stick," he said. Together, van Huis and Dicke helped get mealworms and processed snacks like BugNuggets into the Dutch grocery chain Sligro.

The Dutch are, for reasons of geography, especially concerned about the effects of global warming; they are also progressive when it comes to food development. But entrepreneurs in the United States are starting to explore edible insects, too. Matthew Krisiloff, a student at the University of Chicago, recently started a company called Entom Foods, which is working on deshelling insects using pressurization technology in the hope of selling the meat in cutlet form.

"The problem is the *ick* factor—the eyes, the wings, the legs," he said. "It's not as simple as hiding it in a bug nugget. People won't accept it beyond the novelty. When you think of a chicken you think of a chicken breast, not the eyes, wings, and beak. We're trying to do the same thing with insects, create a stepping-stone, so that when you get a bug nugget you think of the bug steak, not the whole animal." But before he can bring a product to market, he must overcome a daunting technical challenge. Insect protein does not take the form of muscle, but is, as he put it, "goopy."

In Dicke's opinion, simply changing the language surrounding food insects could go a long way toward solving the problem that Westerners have with them. "Maybe we should stop telling people they're eating insects," he said. "If you say it's mealworms, it makes people think of ringworm. So stop saying 'worm.' If we use the Latin names, say it's a *Tenebrio* quiche, it sounds much more fancy, and it's part of the marketing." Another option, Dicke said, is to cover the bugs in chocolate, because people will eat anything covered in chocolate.

.   .   .

The practice of ethical entomophagy started haphazardly. In 1974, Gene DeFoliart, who was the chair of entomology at the University of Wisconsin, was asked by a colleague to recommend someone who could talk about edible insects as part of a symposium on unconventional protein sources. Then, as now, entomology was more concerned with insect eradication than cultivation, and, not finding a willing participant, DeFoliart decided to take on the project himself. He began his talk—and the paper he eventually published—with a startling statement: "C. F. Hodge (1911) calculated that a pair of houseflies beginning operations in April could produce enough flies, if all survived, to cover the earth forty-seven feet deep by August," he said. "If one can reverse for a moment the usual focus on insects as enemies of man, Hodge's layer of flies represents an impressive pile of animal protein."

DeFoliart, who died in early 2013, envisioned a place for edible insects as a luxury item. The larvae of the wax moth (*Galleria mellonella*) seemed to him to be poised to become the next escargot, which in the late eighties represented a three-hundred-million-dollar-a-year business in the United States. "Given a choice, New York diners looking for adventure and willing to pay $22 for half a roasted free-range chicken accompanied by a large pile of shoestring potatoes might well prefer a smaller pile of *Galleria* at the same price," he wrote. He and a handful of colleagues, including Florence Dunkel, now a leading entomophagist and a professor at Montana State University, in Bozeman, began to study and promote the potential of what they called "mini-livestock." In *The Food Insects Newsletter*, their journal, they reported the results of nutritional analyses and assessed the efficiency of insects like crickets—the most delectable of which, entomophagists are fond of pointing out, belong to the genus *Gryllus*.

A couple of years ago, a group of DeFoliart's disciples gathered at a resort in San Diego for a symposium on entomophagy at the annual conference of the Entomological Society of America. Because there is no significant funding available for entomophagy research, it has never been taken seriously by most professional entomologists. Dunkel, who in her half century in academia has many times heard colleagues discourage interested graduate students, often finds herself at odds with others in her field. It was a relief, then, to be among the like-minded. "Your soap-moth-pupae chutney—I'll never forget how that tasted!" she said, introducing a colleague from the Insectarium, in Montreal, which holds a bug banquet every other year. The entomophagists hoped to capitalize on the momentum they perceived. "We don't have to be the kooky, nerdy entomologists who eat bugs because we're crazy," an entomologist from the University of Georgia said. "Twenty years ago, sushi was the *eww* factor; you did not see sushi in grocery stores. Now it's the cultural norm."

At the conference, Dunkel talked about her frustration working in West Africa, where for decades European and American entomologists, through programs like USAID and the British Desert Locust Control Organization, have killed grasshoppers and locusts, which are complete proteins, in order to preserve the incomplete proteins in millet, wheat, barley, sorghum,

and maize. Her field work in Mali focuses on the role of grasshoppers in the diets of children, who, for cultural reasons, do
not eat chicken or eggs. Grasshoppers contain essential amino
acids and serve as a crucial buffer against kwashiorkor, a protein
deficiency that impedes physical and neurological development.
In the village where Dunkel works, kwashiorkor is on the rise;
in recent years, nearby fields have been planted with cotton, and
pesticide use has intensified. Mothers now warn their children
not to collect the grasshoppers, which they rightly fear may be
contaminated.

Mainly, the entomophagists bemoaned the prejudice against
insects. "In our minds, they're associated with filth," Heather
Looy, a psychologist who has studied food aversions, said over
dinner after the symposium. "They go dirty places, but so do
fungi, and we eat those all the time. And you don't want to know
about crabs and shrimp and lobster." Crabs, shrimp, and lobster
are, like insects, arthropods—but instead of eating fresh lettuces
and flowers, as many insects do, they scavenge debris from the
ocean floor.

This injustice—lobster is a delicacy, while vegetarian crustaceans like wood lice are unfit for civilized man—is a centerpiece of the literature of entomophagy. *Why Not Eat Insects?*,
an 1885 manifesto by Vincent M. Holt, which is the founding
document of the movement, expounds upon the vile habits of
the insects of the sea. "The lobster, a creature consumed in in-
credible quantities at all the highest tables in the land, is such
a foul feeder that, for its sure capture, the experienced fisher-
man will bait his lobster-pot with putrid flesh or fish which is
too far gone even to attract a crab," he writes.

As it is, contemporary Westerners tend to associate insects with filth, death, and decay, and, because some insects feed on human blood, their consumption is often seen as cannibalism by proxy. Holt takes pains to stress that the insects he recommends for eating—caterpillars, grasshoppers, slugs—are pure of this taint. "My insects are all vegetable feeders, clean, palatable, wholesome, and decidedly more particular in their feeding than ourselves," he writes. "While I am confident that they will never condescend to eat *us*, I am equally confident that, on finding out how good they are, we shall some day right gladly cook and eat *them*."

Holt's compelling, albeit Swiftian, argument addresses the food problems of his day—"What a pleasant change from the labourer's unvarying meal of bread, lard, and bacon, or bread and lard without bacon, would be a good dish of fried cock-chafers or grasshoppers"—but he is innocent of the nuances of food marketing. Among the sample menus he supplies are offerings like "Boiled Neck of Mutton with Wire-worm Sauce and Moths on Toast." At dinner in San Diego, it occurred to me that this naïveté had carried down. I was sitting next to Lou Sorkin, a forensic entomologist at the American Museum of Natural History who is also an expert on bedbugs, probably the most loathed insect in the United States today. He had arrived at his latest culinary discovery, he said, while experimenting with mediums for preserving maggots collected from murder victims. Realizing that citrus juice might denature proteins as effectively as a chemical solution, and might be more readily available in the field, he soaked large sarcophagid maggots in baths of grapefruit, lemon, lime, and pomelo juice, and *voilà*! Maggot ceviche. "It's a little chewy," he said. "But tasty."

Food preferences are highly local, often irrational, and defining: a Frenchman is a frog because he considers their legs food and the person who calls him one does not. In Santa María Atzompa, a community in Oaxaca where grasshoppers toasted with garlic, chili, and lime are a favorite treat, locals have traditionally found shrimp repulsive. "They would say 'some people' eat it, meaning 'the coastal people,'" Ramona Pérez, an anthropologist at San Diego State University, says. When she made scampi for a family there, she told me, they were appalled; the mother, who usually cooked with her, refused to help, and the daughters wouldn't eat. The coast is less than a hundred miles away.

Eighty percent of the world eats bugs. Australian Aborigines like witchetty grubs, which, according to the authors of *Man Eating Bugs,* taste like "nut-flavored scrambled eggs and mild mozzarella, wrapped in a phyllo dough pastry." Mealworms are factory-farmed in China; in Venezuela, children roast tarantulas. Besides, as any bug-eater will tell you, we are all already eating bugs, whether we mean to or not. According to the FDA, which publishes a handbook on "defect levels" acceptable in processed food, frozen or canned spinach is not considered contaminated until it has fifty aphids, thrips, or mites per hundred grams. Peanut butter is allowed to have thirty insect fragments per hundred grams, and chocolate is OK up to sixty. In each case, the significance of the contamination is given as "aesthetic."

In fresh vegetables, insects are inevitable. One day, cleaning some lettuce, I was surprised by an emerald-green pentagon with antennae: a stinkbug. I got rid of it immediately—force of habit. But daintiness about insects has true consequences. As Tom Turpin, an entomologist at Purdue University, said, "Attitudes in this country result in more pesticide use, because we're scared about an aphid wing in our spinach."

The antipathy that Europeans and their descendants display toward eating insects is stubborn, and mysterious. Insect consumption is in our cultural heritage. The Romans ate beetle grubs reared on flour and wine; ancient Greeks ate grasshoppers. Leviticus, by some interpretations, permits the eating of locusts, grasshoppers, and crickets. (The rest are unkosher.) The manna eaten by Moses on his way out of Egypt is widely believed to have been honeydew, the sweet excrement of scale insects. Turpin thinks it comes down to expedience. Unlike bugs found in the tropics, those found in Europe do not grow big enough to make good food, so there is no culinary tradition, and therefore no infrastructure, to support the practice. He told me, "If there were insects out there the size of pigs, I guarantee you we'd be eating them."

The next stinkbug I came across I ate. It was lightly fried, and presented on a slice of apple, whose flavor it is said to resemble. (I found it a touch medicinal.) This was in a one-story white clapboard house in the West Adams neighborhood of Los Angeles, with a skateboard half-pipe in the backyard. The house had been rented by Daniella Martin and Dave Gracer, two advocates of entomophagy, under false pretenses. "We told them we were scientists," Martin said, giggling. In fact, Martin, who used to be an Internet game-show host, writes a blog called *Girl Meets Bug*; she and Gracer, an English instructor who travels the country lecturing on entomophagy and has been writing an epic poem about insects for the past fourteen years, were in town to compete in a cooking competition at the Natural History Museum's annual bug fair.

Martin, who is in her mid-thirties, with a heart-shaped face and a telegenic smile, stood at the counter in the small kitchen pulling embryonic drones—bee brood—from honeycomb. They were for bee patties, part of a "Bee L T" sandwich she was going to enter in the competition. But, finding them irresistible, she fried up a few to snack on. "It tastes like bacon," she said rapturously. "I'm going to eat the whole plate unless someone gets in there." I did: the drones, dripping in butter and lightly coated with honey from their cells, were fatty and a little bit sweet, and, like everything chitinous, left me with a disturbing aftertaste of dried shrimp.

Gracer opened the freezer and inspected his bugs: housefly pupae, cicadas, and, his favorite, ninety-dollar-a-pound katydids from Uganda. "They're very rich, almost buttery," he said. "They almost taste as if they've gone around the bend."

"Dave, where's the tailless whip scorpion?" Martin said, and Gracer produced an elegantly armored black creature with a foreleg like a calligraphy flourish. "I'm thinking about doing a tempura type of fry and a spicy mayonnaise," Martin, who also worked for a number of years in a Japanese restaurant, said. First, she flash-fried it to soften the exoskeleton, and then she dipped it in tempura batter. To her knowledge, no one had ever before eaten a tailless whip scorpion. "All right, people, let's make history," she said, using a pair of chopsticks to lower it back into the pan, where it sizzled violently. I decided right there on a new policy, one I thought would pass muster with Gold: I will eat disgusting things, but only those with long established culinary traditions.

When the scorpion was finished, she put it on a plate, and she and Gracer sat down on a couch to feast on what looked like far too much bug for me, and yet not nearly enough to satisfy hunger. Gracer pulled off a pincer. "There's something—that white stuff—that's meat!" he cried, pointing to a speck of flesh. "That's meat!" Martin repeated excitedly, and exhorted him to try it. He tasted; she tasted. "Fish," Gracer said. "It has the consistency of fish." Martin split a leg apart and nibbled. In a few bites, they had eaten all there was. "That was really good," she said.

The following morning, in a tent on the front lawn of the Natural History Museum, Gracer faced Zack (the Cajun Bug Chef) Lemann, an established bug-cooker from New Orleans, who dazzled the judges—most of them children—with his "odonate hors d'oeuvres," fried wild-caught dragonflies served on sautéed mushrooms with Dijon-soy butter. Children are often seen as the great hope of entomophagy, because of their openness to new foods, but even they are not without prejudices. Gracer, who presented stinkbug-and-kale salad, had neglected to account for the fact that kids don't like kale.

A five-year-old approached Lemann afterward. "Excuse me, can I eat a dragonfly?" he said. Lemann cooked one for him. The boy picked the batter off, revealing a wing as elaborately paned as a cathedral window, and then bit into it: his first bug. His little brother, who was three, came over and asked for a bite. "Good," he pronounced.

"Who's going to eat the head?" their mother asked.

"I will," the five-year-old said. "Once somebody licks the mustard off."

The last round of the day matched Martin against Gracer. He was making Ugandan-katydid-and-grilled-cheese sandwiches. Drawing on her Japanese-restaurant experience, Martin decided to make a spider roll, using a rose-haired tarantula bought from a pet store. She held up the spider and burned off its hair with a lighter, and then removed its abdomen. "The problem with eating an actual spider roll, made with crab, is that they're bottom feeders," she said. "This spider probably ate only crickets, which ate only grass." She whipped up a sauce and added a few slices of cucumber, and then presented her dish to the judges, warning them brightly to "be very careful of the fangs!"

A young girl with curly hair lunged eagerly at the plate. "If it's in sushi, I'll eat it," she said. When she had tried a piece, she declared, "It's sushi. With spiders. It's awesome."

Four-fifths of the animal species on earth are insects, and yet food insects are not particularly easy to find. Home cooks can call Fred Rhyme, of Rainbow Mealworms, who provided the Madagascar hissing cockroaches for *Fear Factor*. He sells more than a billion worms a year; the sign at the edge of his farm, a conglomeration of twenty-three trailers, shotgun houses, and former machine shops in South Los Angeles, says, "Welcome to Worm City, Compton, Cal., 90220½. Population:

990,000,000." The farm supplies six hundred thousand worms a week to the San Diego Zoo. "It's mostly animals we feed," Rhyme's wife, Betty, who is the company's president, told me. "The people are something of an oddity."

I wasn't in the market for more mealworms. I had gone to visit Florence Dunkel, the entomologist, in Montana, and eaten plenty of them, fried up in butter, in her kitchen. They smelled of mushrooms and tasted of sunflower seeds. The flavor was unobjectionable, but not reason enough to eat something that reminded me of the time I was halfway through a sleeve of extra-crumbly Ritz crackers before I realized that the crumbs were moving. I wanted to see if bugs could be transcendent, and I knew who would know. "One of the biggest successes of the local New Cocktailian movement is the mezcal-based Donaji at Rivera downtown, which Julian Cox serves in a rocks glass rimmed with toasted-grasshopper salt," Jonathan Gold wrote to me. I duly went to the restaurant and ordered the Donaji, a $14 cocktail named after a Zapotec princess. The salt tasted like Jane's Krazy Mixed-Up Salt, crushed Bac-Os, and fish-food flakes; the bartender recommended it as a rub for grilled meat.

Gold also mentioned that I might try Laurent Quenioux, at Bistro LQ, an old acquaintance of his. Gold's 2006 review of Quenioux's wild hare stew—"a soft, gloriously stinky Scottish hare stewed in something approximating the traditional *foie gras*–inflected blood"—was one of the pieces for which he won the Pulitzer. To me, Gold wrote, "He occasionally has *escamoles*, giant ant eggs, on the menu. They're very seasonal, early spring I think, so you'd have to call." It was winter. I would have to wait.

Escamoles are not actually eggs but immature *Liometopum*

apiculatum. A delicacy since Aztec times—they were used as tribute to Moctezuma—they are still a prized ingredient in high-end Mexico City restaurants, where they are known colloquially as Mexican caviar. Exquisitely subtle, palest beigy-pink, knobbly as a seed pearl, they command a market price of around $70 a pound.

Like humans, *Liometopum apiculatum* ants are opportunists; they will eat anything they can overpower, and, because they do not sting, they tear their prey to shreds. (They are also ranchers, tending flocks of aphids and defending them from lady beetles, in exchange for the aphids' surplus honeydew.) They burrow under boulders or at the base of trees, and live in colonies of up to fifty thousand members. Traditionally, they were hunted only by experienced *escamoleros*—the irrepressible image is of an ant with a Tejano hat with a lasso—but, according to Julieta Ramos-Elorduy, a biologist who studies food insects at the National Autonomous University of Mexico, their desirability has invited poachers, who overharvest and destroy the nests. The ants, which are most readily available in the state of Hidalgo, are also found in the southwestern United States. High prices have inspired North American foragers to get in on the business. "Recently at San Juan market in Mexico City, monopolizers informed us that small airplanes loaded with tons of the product arrived from the United States and sold it to the highest bidders," Ramos-Elorduy wrote in a 2006 paper.

You can't really buy *escamoles* in America. The head chef at José Andrés's Oyamel, in D.C., has scoured local markets for them without success, though once, on a tip from a lady who overheard him complaining to his barber about their unavailability, he discovered some frozen Thai ant larvae (labeled as "puffed rice") in an Asian grocery store in Virginia. José Andrés himself told me that he considers *escamoles* a delicacy, and if he could get them he'd put them on the menu at Minibar, his acclaimed six-seat restaurant.

At the first sign of spring, I called Quenioux. He had just closed Bistro LQ because of a problem with the lease, and said he was trying to get some *escamoles* to serve at Starry Kitchen, a downtown lunch counter owned by Nguyen and Thi Tran, who had previously run it as an underground supper club out of their apartment. Quenioux was about to start a pop-up there called LQ@SK. "Basically, you need to smuggle them," he said of the ants. His connection, a Mexican man living near Hidalgo who brought them in foam cups in his carry-on luggage, didn't work anymore; the last two times Quenioux had placed an order, he'd prepaid, only to have his shipment confiscated by Customs at LAX.

A week before the soft launch of Quenioux's residency at Starry Kitchen, he told me that he had a line on some *escamoles*. He knew a guy who knew a guy who would bring them across the border from Tijuana; we simply had to drive down to a meeting place on the U.S. side and escort them back. We set a time, and I went to a street corner in Pasadena, near where Quenioux lives; when I arrived, a red Toyota Corolla was waiting. The window came down partway, and I heard someone call my name.

Originally from Sologne, France, Quenioux—pronounced "kin*you*"—grew up hunting, learned pastry in Paris at Maxim's, and worked in Nice alongside the German-born chef Joachim Splichal, who brought him to Los Angeles in the early eighties.

He is a gentle person, with huge, pale green eyes, a bald-shaved head, a set of prayer beads around his wrist, and the endearingly antisocial habit of seeing everything he encounters as potential food: the deer near Mt. Wilson, which he hunts with a bow and arrow; the purple blossoms of the jacaranda trees; a neighbor's chicken, which he killed and cooked when it came into his yard. Usually, he eats chicken only when he's home in France; he thinks American chickens are disgusting.

Certain laws just don't make sense to Quenioux, like the one that prohibits him from serving a dessert made from chocolate hot-boxed with pot smoke. "What's one gram of marijuana, just to have the smoke infuse the chocolate?" he said. When he read in the news that there was to be a mass culling of fifty thousand wild boars that had crossed from Texas into Chihuahua and were destroying everything in their path—not fit for consumption, warned a government official—his first thought was, Shit, can we get a few of those? "Tamales!" Daniel, his sous-chef, said. "With salsa verde!"

As for the *escamoles*, "We do it for the culinary adventure," Quenioux said. He has made blinis with ant eggs and caviar, and a three-egg dish of *escamoles*, quail eggs, and salmon roe. He has fantasized about making an *escamole* quiche, and, using just the albumen that drains out when the eggs are frozen, meringue. His signature dish is a corn tortilla resting on a nasturtium leaf and topped with *escamoles* sautéed in butter with epazote, shallots, and serrano chilies, served with a shot of Mexican beer and a lime gel. Insects are, to him, like any other ingredient: a challenge and an invitation. "Let's do gastronomy with bugs," he said. "Let's make something delicious."

Quenioux talked about *escamoles* all the way down south—their delicate eggy qualities, their wildness, their unexpected appearance ("condensed milk with little pebbles in it"), the responsibility he feels to train the American palate to accept them. "The insects will be the solution to feed all those masses, but how do you get insects on the daily table in America?" he said. "In the last twenty years, we grew here in America from iceberg lettuce to baby frisée, so the time is now."

After a few hours, we arrived at a strip mall and parked in front of a drugstore, then walked toward the meeting place, a restaurant, where the *escamoles* were waiting. "OK, let's go," Quenioux said, getting out of the car. "I've got the cash."

The front door to the restaurant was open, and an old man with a drooping moustache was mopping the floor. "Hola, *señor*," Quenioux said. The old man pointed to a Dutch door, which led to the kitchen. Quenioux stuck his head in, and eventually a young woman wearing a dirty chef's coat and a white apron appeared. "You come for the *escamoles*?" she said. "OK, I get for you." She returned a minute later with a plastic shopping bag containing a large ziplock filled with half a kilo of frozen product. Quenioux handed her a hundred-dollar bill.

Getting back in the car, Quenioux opened the bag to examine the goods, a pale orange slush, scattered with clumps of oblong ant babies. "We got the loot!" he squealed.

The Starry Kitchen narrative, with its elements of amateurism, scofflaw pluck, and media savvy, is the kind of restaurant story you hear all the time these days. In 2009, when Thi

Tran lost her job in advertising, she asked her Facebook friends what she should do. "Cook, cook, cook," came the reply. Thi is first-generation Chinese, with a natural scowl. She is practical and modest, where her husband, Nguyen, who is Vietnamese-American, is boisterous. He often dresses up in Comic-Con-style costumes for food events, and displays a sign, referring to a spicy tofu dish that is a Starry Kitchen specialty, which reads "Eat My Balls."

Inspired by Kogi—the Korean-barbecue food truck that started in L.A. and set off a national craze—Thi thought Vietnamese tacos might be good, and developed some recipes at home. Three weeks later, Nguyen told her, "We're serving out of our apartment this Sunday," and flyered their three-hundred-unit building in North Hollywood. To him it was normal: like a lot of Asians he knows, he grew up eating in unofficial home restaurants. "In every ethnic neighborhood in L.A. there is someone doing something like this," he said.

Within a few months, their apartment was the No. 1 rated Asian fusion restaurant on Yelp. (Providence, a fantastically expensive restaurant with two Michelin stars, was No. 2.) When the health department confronted Nguyen with the Twitter feed where he shamelessly touted specials and warned him to stop, Thi was unnerved, but Nguyen insisted that the intervention was a blessing. They moved the restaurant, which they had named after a popular Hong Kong cooking show, into a legitimate space in a large corporate plaza, and burnished their creation myth. "It increased our audience," he told me. "We were seedy, and being caught validated that we really *were* underground."

A week after the ant run, I was at Starry Kitchen, watching

Quenioux get ready to serve the *escamoles* as an *amuse-bouche*. Nguyen bounded around, talking about his role in securing them. "I called everyone, from Laos, Cambodia, Thailand—all the sources I know got caught," he said. He was thrilled about the air of the forbidden that the dish would confer. "It's going to be a great note to start on—not even the taste, just them knowing it was smuggled and it's ant eggs," he said.

To complement a menu full of Asian flavors—teriyaki rabbit meatballs in miso broth, veal sweetbreads with shishito peppers and yuzu—Quenioux had decided to prepare the *escamoles* with Thai basil and serve them with Sapporo. "These are very spicy," he said, placing an ample green nasturtium leaf on a plate. "I foraged them from my garden this morning." There was a light sheen of sweat on his forehead.

Just before the service, the waiters started to panic. "What am I telling them?" one asked. "I can't just go up to them and say it's ant eggs."

"Tell them it's very exotic, and traditional in Mexico City," Daniel, the sous-chef, said. I went into the dining room and sat down. "This is an *amuse* from the chef," a waiter said, presenting me with the dish, a composition as spare and earthy as a Japanese garden. "It's smuggled-in ant eggs." I rolled the leaf around the tortilla and bit: peppery nasturtium, warm tortilla, and then the light pop of *escamoles* bursting like tiny corn kernels. A whiff of dirt, a sluice of beer, and that was it. They were gone by night's end, but their fresh, succulent sweetness stuck with me. Unexpectedly, I had something new to crave.

Three

BACKDOOR MEN

I got in 2K live crickets," Brett Ottolenghi, the ostentatiously earnest, honest, perpetually worried young proprietor of Artisanal Foods, a fancy-food purveyor in Las Vegas, wrote me by text message. "Thinking I'd try to cook with them before offering to chefs. But the pen I made isn't working and they are escaping by the hundreds in my house." Five minutes later, he wrote me again. "I think I'll have to live among them. There is no way I can pick up this many. A Chinese chef might help me cook some tomorrow."

Las Vegas is among the top food cities in America, if you go by the number of superexpensive restaurants with famous chefs. Ten of the fifty highest-grossing restaurants in the country are on the Strip, and there are more master sommeliers in Las Vegas than in any other city in the country. Adam Carmer, the casino developer Steve Wynn's first hotel sommelier, described himself to me as "the No. 1 maître d' in town." He says, "Other places, you might have four or five extraordinary restaurants in a state or in a country; here you have four or five in a hotel. For shoes, you go to the mall—that's what the food's like out here." Almost forty million people visited Las Vegas last year. It is one of the places in the world where the outlandish ideas and hyperprecious ingredients of the food avant-garde meet the masses, and Ottolenghi is one of the people making introductions.

Ottolenghi specializes in the small run, the vaguely regulated, the hard to come by, and the about to be banned. He carries Utah clay, fresh Pennsylvania hops, and squid ink from Spain. One of his newest products, which he has yet to place, is *kopi luwak*—coffee beans gathered from civet droppings. The beans, which have an exquisite burnt caramel flavor, are extremely rare and can cost as much as $1,000 a pound. "I have some of the turds," he told me, which makes presentations lively. He often says that he is on a first-name basis with three hundred and seventy chefs in Vegas—the executive chefs and sous-chefs and chefs de cuisine at Jean Georges Steakhouse, Le Cirque, Daniel Boulud, barMASA, and dozens more—by which he may mean that he has forgotten their last names, or, if they are French, is unsure how to pronounce them. To the chefs, he is "the truffle kid"—for his first product, which he started selling online when he was thirteen—or Hamleg, owing to his tendency to walk through casino lobbies carrying the hairy, hoof-on hindquarters of a pig.

Because of its primary identity, as a place to gamble, Las Vegas attracts some of the broadest eaters in the world: high-rolling Asian whales. There are some who say that if the casinos were to stop serving shark-fin soup in the high-limit rooms—where it goes for $100 to $300 a bowl—the city's economy would collapse. But shark fin, a slippery, flavorless textural delight that is the pièce de résistance of formal Chinese banquets, is condemned by many as cruel and unsustainable. Sharks, whose numbers, including that of the "soupfin," have diminished severely, are often de-finned live and then dumped back in the ocean to bleed out, get eaten, or drown. California outlawed shark fin in 2013, and there are efforts under way to ban it in Vegas. This is the kind of crisis that Ottolenghi calls an opportunity.

Among the many impostors in the food business, he hunts for authenticity. Don't get him started on what passes, in most people's minds, for cinnamon: the great majority of it is mislabeled cassia. He gets the real thing from its only source, Sri Lanka. But when it comes to shark fin, inauthenticity is exactly what he's looking for. He has found a company in China that takes tilapia tails—tail, like fin, is cartilage—and makes a faux shark-fin product that is identical in taste, texture, and appearance. There is just one obstacle: the customer. The whales, he says, want the real thing *because* it's rare. His next idea is to use sturgeon tails, which might prove desirable due to their prestigious association with caviar.

Ottolenghi prides himself on the fulfillment of outrageous and obscure demands. He has sourced pink pine nuts for Alessandro Stratta, the chef at Alex and at Stratta, two fine-dining restaurants in Las Vegas. "Just put them in my mailbox," I heard him say to a tortilla-and-chili dealer who had located some in New Mexico. One Chinese New Year, he furnished the buffet at the Bellagio with four hundred pounds of fatted duck breast on less than twenty-four hours' notice. After the authorities forced Guy Savoy, a two-Michelin-star restaurant at Caesars Palace, to remove a popular guinea-hen-in-pig-bladder dish from its menu—the bladder was coming from a non-USDA-approved source—the restaurant turned to Ottolenghi. "They still get tons of requests for it, so they gave me the mission of trying to get domestic pig bladders," he says. He called pig farms and slaughter-houses in four states. "I really exhausted every possibility. There's no way to get a pig bladder in this country—they're all ground up for dog food."

Several years ago, Ludo Lefebvre, the dashing, volatile French chef who invented the pop-up restaurant and became a tele-vision star, was cooking at a restaurant in Las Vegas. He asked Ottolenghi for *piment d'Espelette*, a subtle chili pepper. *Piment d'Espelette* is rare; the *zone de l'appellation*, in southwestern France, is only a few thousand acres. In powder form, the pepper can wholesale for $110 a pound. (Paprika is less than $8.) After ini-tially working through an importer, Ottolenghi had decided to become one himself, making him, by his count, the third importer of *piment d'Espelette* to the United States.

That is how he came to spend a drizzly afternoon in the spring of 2010 in the tiny Basque town of Ainhoa, quizzing a young farmer named Claire about her production methods. Claire, who had rosy cheeks and a rippled Gallic nose dotted with moles, explained that they used only *pesticide biologique*, good bugs to eat bad ones. Chickens pecked among white plaster buildings with red tile roofs and peeling black shutters: Ainhoa's single architectural gesture. Claire invited us into one of the buildings and prepared a pepper tasting. As she swirled the powder in a little stemmed glass, causing it to clink—"Can you hear? It's very dry," she said—she explained the properties she controlled for. The color should be a rich, oxygenated red, and the flavor, ideally, is a balance of fruitiness, toastiness, and *foin,* an aftertaste of hay. A Basque passenger of Columbus's, Claire said, had brought the pepper back from the New World.

The next day, Ottolenghi had a lunch appointment in La Alberca, six hundred kilometers away, at the headquarters of Fermín, the only Spanish producer of Ibérico ham approved by the USDA for sale in the United States. Ottolenghi was the exclusive source for Fermín products in Las Vegas. He woke at eight o'clock, checked the map, and set out optimistically. I had already been traveling with him for a few days and was afraid—of his navigation and of my endurance. Food people either stuff you or starve you. Ottolenghi, an ascetic, is a starver. At home, he often consumes little more than a kefir-and-raw-egg shake in a day. On the first night of our trip, we had stayed in San Sebastián, the Michelin three-star capital of the world, and I found myself alone at dinnertime, eating a grim vegetarian patty in the hotel dining room. Driving to La Alberca, we passed dozens of small towns and scores of restaurants without stopping to eat. I devoured bags of filling-station peanuts and, by the fistful, a loaf of soft gingerbread I had picked up in Ainhoa the night before.

In the late afternoon, we turned off the highway and onto a small road that hugged a mossy stone wall decked with wild red poppies and fried-egg flowers. On the other side was an oak forest. Young bulls bound for the ring relaxed in the shade. It was past four when we arrived in La Alberca, a pork-centric place where the hanging limbs and loins of cured Ibérico pigs serve as decoration for the tapas bars, and outside the church there is a statue of a boar, like a local saint. Just past town, we found the Fermín plant, an elegant structure built in the mid-eighties whose style referred to the area's medieval history: fieldstone facing, held in place by a loose lattice of half-timbers. Raúl Martín, a grand-nephew of the founder, led us down to a basement dining hall with tiled floors and an open fireplace, where Luis, a jug-eared cook with a double chin, was grilling cuts of pig meat: tenderloin, pancetta, ribs, *pluma* ("feather," or loin tip), *presa* (collar), and *secreto,* a cut hidden away between the ribs and the fat. Rich smoke filled the air.

Ibérico meat is unctuous—up to 35 percent fat—and its most luxurious variety, *bellota* (acorn), melts at room temperature. Bellota pigs, which are released into the forest in the fall to hunt for acorns, are so oily that they are known as "olive trees with legs." Last year, Fermín slaughtered only five thousand bellota pigs, for a total of ten thousand hams, ten thousand shoulders. The hams cure for three years; the shoulders, which are bonier, take at least two. Retail shops charge $130 a pound for the ham. Bellota is what sells in Las Vegas.

Martín showed the way to a long wooden table piled with breadbaskets and wine and trays of chorizo and *salsichon.* Javier, a Fermín employee, joined us, and everyone started to gossip about ham, as Luis brought over platter after platter of cooked meat and Ottolenghi stood at an iron *jamonera,* cutting thin slices of bellota for the group.

"We sent today a bellota to the royal palace, for the heads of state of Europe," Javier said. Ottolenghi nodded, and told an equivalent story of Las Vegas aristocracy. Had the Spaniards heard of Cirque du Soleil? Yes, Martín said. "Every Christmas, Guy Laliberté, who started it, buys three bellota legs from Robuchon's L'Atelier," Ottolenghi reported. Then Martín held up a vacuum-packed shank. "This is one of José Andrés's ideas," he said. (The chef is an importer for Fermín.) "It's 'corderico'— Ibérico-style lamb, fed on acorns and dried. This is the only one in the world."

Early the following morning, we watched the pigs get cleaned, stunned, cut, and hung on hooks from tracks that traced loops on the ceiling. Large men chiseled at them as if they were blocks of stone from which something more aesthetically pleasing could be coaxed. Then Martín showed us the room where the hams were cured—he called it "the bank"—and the breeding farm, so that we could see the Ibéricos alive. They had thick black hides, like toy rhinos, and brayed mournfully as they rutted and fought. A farmworker handed Ottolenghi several acorns of the variety that the bellota gorge on in the forest. Seeing an opportunity to impress his chefs with the depth of his knowledge, he pocketed them. Leaving Fermín, Ottolenghi asked me if I'd ever read *The Jungle*. "It's my favorite book," he said. "It's all about how efficient the meat business is at using every part."

Ottolenghi, a Millennial-generation foodie who grew up watching exotic-food shows on TV, comes from mushroom people. His parents, Arturo and Hannah, seed the logs in their backyard in Gettysburg, Pennsylvania, with shiitakes; morels and chanterelles grow wild. Once, when the family was living in Ohio, before Brett was born and when his brother, Alex, was an infant, Arturo spotted a hardwood forest out the car window. Suspecting that it could be harboring chanterelles, he pulled over and found two solid acres of them. As Arturo tells it, "I picked a few, took them home, and called Chanterelle, in New York, and asked for the owner. I said, 'I know this sounds crazy, but I'm in Ohio and I have some fresh chanterelles—do you want five to ten pounds?' She said, 'Whatever you can ship. Anything I don't use, my friends at Dean & DeLuca will use.' Hannah and I parked Alex in a cradle with a mosquito net over it and packed up as many boxes as we could, took them to the airport, and that same evening all over lower Manhattan people were eating our chanterelles."

On a family trip to San Francisco, when Brett was twelve, he ordered a pasta dish with truffle oil on it. This led to a conversation about the high price of truffles in the United States. At the time, there was only one major importer, Urbani, an old Italian company that still dominates the market. Brett decided to see if he could compete. He was already something of an entrepreneur. In second grade, he sold Pixy Stix and gourmet lollipops at school, in violation of campus rules, and was sent to the principal's office. In seventh, he started importing laser pens from China for eleven dollars and selling them for twenty, and wound up in the principal's office again.

Brett and Arturo started the Truffle Market, an online venture selling truffles that they imported from Italy, in 1998. When *Newsweek* mentioned that their company was selling white truffles for $60 an ounce, compared with Dean & DeLuca's price of $106 for the same amount, business increased tenfold. "I was making thirty percent on it and I thought it was great," Brett says now. "I didn't even know that was a small profit." With perishable products, you have to make a killing; at some point you will inevitably lose a shipment to spoilage or to overeager Customs officials. Brett remembers that Fareed Zakaria placed an order, as did the actor Heath Ledger. Robert Mondavi, the winemaker, began to use the Ottolenghi mushrooms for his truffle parties. But the Ottolenghis' best customer was a young woman in Palm Beach, referred by the manager of the Palm Beach Country Club, who ordered a pound of white truffles a week for the entire season, September through December. She hated truffles, but a business associate of her father's, an oil executive from Houston, liked to fly to Palm Beach for the weekends, and he expected to have a plate of them waiting on his bedside table. He ate them like apples.

In the food business, Brett found youth to be an inconvenience. Rather than present the Truffle Market as a father-son venture, as Arturo had hoped, Brett insisted that his father pose alone for the picture in their first catalog. "To buy a truffle from a guy named Arturo Ottolenghi, that makes sense," Brett says. "Not from Brett, who's thirteen." For a while, he styled himself "J. Brett Ottolenghi" on his business cards. When he expanded the Truffle Market and renamed it Artisanal Foods, in 2008, he used an unsmiling picture of himself, sporting a suit jacket, a three-day beard, and a pair of fake eyeglasses, which he likes to wear for work, particularly when he's meeting a chef for the first time. "I probably have twenty pairs," he says.

Arturo's Italian background was Brett's great good fortune. Arturo's maternal great-great-grandfather had been the Prussian consul general to the Kingdom of the Two Sicilies; he found oil in Indonesia and sold out to John D. Rockefeller in 1900. The Ottolenghis were Italian Jews who converted to Catholicism during the war and donated a set of bronze doors to St. Peter's Basilica. Growing up in New York, Arturo went by the name Milton, but he spent his summers at a large family property in Piedmont, where he developed a taste for white truffles, as well as the language skills that would come in handy when bargaining for them later on his son's behalf. Arturo now runs a business that provides sandpaper to body shops and woodworkers. "I only work with consumables," he says.

For tenth grade, Brett went to St. Andrew's, a boarding school in Delaware. To keep the Truffle Market going, he rented storage space from Arturo and paid his employees to pack and ship. From school, he handled orders and did the bookkeeping. Soon mushroom hunters all over the world were e-mailing him—Serbs and Croats and Chinese, primarily. Someone from Egypt sent him a box of the inexpensive, sandy desert truffles known as *terfez*. Foragers in Oregon sent him white truffles they had found, which he cooked up with scrambled eggs for the whole school. The school cook was his closest friend; they once ordered an alligator, grilled it, and served it in the dining room.

The Croatian truffles were a revelation: the same species as the rarest and most expensive white Italians—*Tuber magnatum*—but not subject to the 100 percent tariff imposed on truffles entering the United States from the European Union. They became the Truffle Market's main product. Brett left St. Andrew's and finished high school at Mercersburg Academy, another boarding school, which was in Pennsylvania and closer to home. While there, he became an importer of Mogu pillows from Japan, and befriended local cheese-makers, who would deliver samples to his dorm room.

Ottolenghi moved to Las Vegas in 2004, to attend UNLV's William F. Harrah College of Hotel Administration. He stored truffles in his room, offending his hallmates with the smell, and kept his cell phone on vibrate while in class, to field orders. Carless, he walked up and down the Strip with a little basket of truffles and a scale, making unannounced visits to chefs at the best restaurants and trying to talk them into buying an expensive luxury ingredient from a baby-faced, bespectacled nineteen-year-old freshman, sweating in his suit.

Storytelling may be the one indispensable skill in food-selling, but the richest histories of ingredients like those that Ottolenghi deals in tend to be suppressed. Ottolenghi once found beautiful *huitlacoche*—corn fungus—on a thirteen-acre farm in Florida. "All my family used to be in the citrus business," the farmer told me when I called. "Then one night it got down to ten degrees. First they went broke, then they got dead. I was Br'er Bear at Disneyworld. Then I was a bartender. Then I got divorced and had to run away from my wife. *Huitlacoche* was my brother's idea. We started doing it together, then we got in a fight and now I'm doing it on my own."

Wild products often come with even more obscure pedigrees. Huckleberries, fiddleheads, lichens, ramps, ferns, and, of

course, mushrooms, are largely unregulated, potentially dangerous, fragile, precious, and scarce. Finding them is a scrounge.
Often they represent stolen goods; a great deal of foraging takes
place on government and private land, unpermitted. Iso Rabins
is a sometime mushroom picker who ran San Francisco's Underground Market—part church bake sale, part faerie bazaar, a
place where you could buy DIY rearing-and-grinding mealworm kits—until the health department shut him down. He
told me, "Once a chanterelle gets into Rainbow Grocery in San
Francisco it has this elitist air of a clean, pure, product from
the mountains, untouched by man." The truth, he said, is often
less savory: tweakers driving dirty pickups into the national forest, mushroom buckets rattling around with the old beer cans.
"Meth is a really good drug if you want to forage all the time,"
Rabins said. "If you want to spend forty-eight hours looking at
the ground, meth does a good job." A major West Coast mushroom buyer told me that professional pickers tend to be "feral
types." He said he once turned on the news to see a guy he'd
been using for a couple of years named a Most Wanted Person.

Commercial foraging is largely subsistence work for mar-
ginal people with little connection to the gourmet status of the
forest products they are gathering. Sometimes they may not
even recognize their yield as edible. One Sunday in the winter
of 2012, Belinda and Dan Conne, a couple in their late forties,
went with their twenty-five-year-old son, Michael, and their
pit bull, Jesse, into the Rogue River–Siskiyou National Forest,
a wilderness area outside Gold Beach, Oregon, to pick black
trumpets and hedgehogs. The Connes, who did obtain a permit, were amateurs, recent transplants from Oklahoma who had

come to Gold Beach in search of work but found little available by the time they arrived in July. They moved into a tent at a campground and eventually into a camper with no electrical or water hookups. Belinda cleaned motel rooms for a few hours a week; Dan, scraggly-haired, tattooed, and missing several of his top teeth, had a back injury and couldn't work.

A neighbor in camp, seeing that they were struggling, taught Michael how to hunt for mushrooms—in addition to the black trumpets and hedgehogs, they found yellow feet, candy caps, and "channies"—which they sold to the local agent for a big mushroom buyer. (The agent they sold to, a Czech forager in his late fifties, pleaded guilty to trespassing in 2006, after being charged with using GPS to poach chanterelles from ranches in Lompoc. His advice to me: Don't get arrested in Santa Barbara County.) For black trumpets, a picker usually gets about five bucks a pound from a buyer, who marks them up 30 percent and sells them to a wholesaler, which sells them for 30 percent more to a retailer, which, depending on the season, doubles or quadruples the price and puts them on the shelves. A typical haul brought the Connes $50, enough to fill their car with gas, buy some propane, and get a few days' worth of groceries. "We did this so we could survive," Belinda told me.

The Connes were having a good day, and, after emptying their buckets into bags in the car, decided to go back out again. Just as they got to a patch of trumpets it started to rain, and the woods grew dark. "We got up on them blacks," Belinda said. "What we did, we were on the trail of the blacks, and we got greedy. We kept picking." When they looked up, they realized they didn't know where they were. "It kept raining harder, getting darker and darker, so we bedded down for the night," she said. Their lean-to collapsed in the storm. In the morning, it was still raining, and the Connes found that they were in the old growth, with no path out. Michael found a fallen tree, rotting and spacious enough for the three of them to sit inside; he hollowed a section of it clean with his knife, and they all crammed in, filling in the chinks with sticks and leaves so they wouldn't get wet. When afternoon came, they pulled large pieces of bark across the opening.

The last thing the Connes had eaten was a batch of peanut butter sandwiches on Sunday afternoon. In the tree, all night, they talked about food. Someone indelicately brought up the Donner Party. They watched big timber ants crawl along the inside of the log. "We thought about poppin' the heads off and eating them that way," Belinda said, adding that the wiggling of a live one would have been too much for her. "That's a last resort. The worms I don't think I could ever do." As for mushrooms, white buttons from the grocery store were the only kind they ate. Dan tried a hedgehog and spat it out; it was his first taste of the delicacy that had lured his family to the woods, and he found it repulsive. "My husband said if we come down to starvin' that we could eat them," Belinda said. His other idea—eat Jesse—was overruled. "Michael and I said we would take one of our legs first," Belinda said. "I would starve to death before I could eat a dog. A squirrel? Yes, I could. But a *dog*?" They placed all their hopes on rescue.

Dan's back hurt so badly that he couldn't move. Michael fell in the creek while collecting water in a ziplock bag and developed hypothermia. The frostbite on his feet turned to trench. Belinda, who also had frostbite, watched her son grow weaker, and was sure that he was going to die. On Thursday, Dan turned to her and said, "Today's the day when they're going to start notifying the next of kin." They listened to the helicopters overhead and tried in vain to signal them with the face of a dead cell phone and the blade of a buck knife. Still, for six days they didn't eat a thing, until—on the day before the search mission would have changed from rescue to recovery—they were spotted and flown to a hospital. Grateful to have escaped with his life, Dan broke his fast with pepperoni sticks and Doritos.

The world Brett operates in, it's a lot of backdoor bullshit and making deals," an old Vegas hand and a friend of Ottolenghi's said. Corruption is rampant. "You'll have a food-and-beverage VP that goes with a certain purveyor because he says, 'I'll sell you crab legs for the buffet and write you a personal check for ten percent of whatever we do. You'll make two hundred and fifty grand because you buy two and a half million in crab.'" Another chef told me about a couple of fast-talking local seafood venders, an Italian who looks Spanish and a Spaniard who looks Italian. "They have very raspy voices, like something out of a scene in a Mafia movie," he said. "They do this bait-and-switch thing, telling you stories, and before you know it there's a thousand pounds of tuna waiting at your back door."

Las Vegas's Butter Man, Clint Arthur, says, "It's very cutthroat." He sells 85-percent-butterfat butter to the chefs at Aureole, Payard, Jean Georges Steakhouse, and Restaurant Guy Savoy, and once designed an extra-salty butter for David

Werly, the executive chef at Le Cirque. "The thing you have to understand is that food is a perishable item; it must be purchased, and someone is going to make money on it. These deals typically last for years, they're worth hundreds of thousands of dollars, and people resort to extreme measures, including sometimes illegal measures, to try to get clients. I've seen high-end chefs in Las Vegas fired for taking money under the table from suppliers."

As the Butter Man, Arthur, who is also the author of a series of inspirational lectures on how to double your income, goes to chef meetings dressed in a button-down shirt in "butter yellow" and a pair of yellow Crocs. Most of the vegetable exotica in town comes from Lee Jones, who has a family farm in Huron, Ohio, where he raises rhubarb "the thickness of three pencil leads," miniature cucumbers with tiny yellow blossoms, and heirloom champagne ice beets, for sorbets. His produce travels by FedEx and is ready to be served within twenty-four hours of harvest. When he comes to Las Vegas himself, he is Farmer Lee, and wears the uniform he has trademarked with the U.S. Attorney General's office: dark blue overalls, white shirt, red bow tie. "It's the authentic real deal," he says. "Colonel Sanders has the white suit and the goatee. Dave Thomas, the founder of Wendy's, always wore a short-sleeve shirt. It gives us an identity."

The city's senior caviar purveyor is Barry Katcher—or Barry Beluga, as he calls himself—who has been selling to the casinos for more than twenty years. His family started in caviar in 1942, when his grandfather and great-uncle emigrated from Russia to Brooklyn. His great-uncle, a cobbler, sold it from a shoeshine box in front of a relative's pharmacy, and came to be known as the Caviar Baron. Caviar Royale, Katcher's company, is, he says, the largest supplier to the hotel-casino industry in the United States. I went to see him—petite and deeply tanned, in late middle age, wearing black down to a pair of platform Skechers—at his retail store, on a stretch of Industrial Road behind Caesars Palace. "Everyone should know where it is," he told me, when I asked for directions. "When the cabs bring customers here to buy liquor I give them a free sandwich." His nickname, he said, originated with a radio personality whose show he used to call in to while making his runs to the airport at 3:30 a.m. "Once, I was sent an illegal shipment of caviar—the guys that got it got it illegally—and I said, 'Hey, I've got seven cars around me with blue markings and their lights on.' It was the FDA. They followed me back here and in front of them I opened twenty tins. It was all live on the air." Katcher sees perfidy everywhere: two-faced purchasing agents, fake beluga, competitors who bribe buyers or—worse—milk him for information and then try to take his customers. "See all these knives in my back?" he said. When I mentioned that Ottolenghi had started representing caviar, he winced and said, "Piece of shit."

The pitch that Ottolenghi makes is for integrity, a posture he communicates with unfashionable brown suits, brown leather shoes, and the fake glasses. "It's a very specific look," he says. "Almost professorial." Being well, if humbly, dressed prevents him from getting stopped by security while sneaking around the back corridors of casinos. "Look like you're supposed to be here," he told me, ineffectually, as we skulked around. Besides, light suits in Las Vegas say VIP host (the slick fixers employed by nightclubs to cater to important customers), which doesn't inspire the trust of chefs. He thinks of himself as an educator and a reformer—teaching chefs about the virtues of the products he is selling, not to mention what is wrong with the wares of his competitors—and prides himself on his bold moves. When he knew that the venerable French chef Joël Robuchon would be in town because one of his restaurants had ordered six of Ottolenghi's bellota hams for a party, he dropped in on him, hoping to present a Spanish caviar that he had recently added to his inventory. "I just gave Chef Robuchon the caviar sample despite not having a meeting," he wrote me in a gleeful text message. "Everyone was looking at me as if I had interrupted the Pope."

Caviar—so dear, so highly controlled, so easily concealed—is the cocaine of food. It comes from the virgin eggs of sturgeon, prehistoric fish of massive proportions. The beluga, or *Huso huso*, is the biggest; it can grow to more than three thousand pounds, and live for a hundred years. The Caspian Sea once teemed with them; in the early nineteenth century, a twenty-four-foot-long female was caught in the Volga estuary.

People have been preserving sturgeon eggs for millennia; for the Phoenicians, they were a food of famine. But by the mid-twentieth century, caviar was a luxury good, an extra-special specialty item. "Even the Russians took part," noted a report on the second Fancy Food Show, in 1956. "They displayed caviar aimed at exciting the palates of capitalists." It takes around fifteen years for a sturgeon to mature. Theocracies and dictators were good beluga stewards, but with the dissolution of the Soviet Union in the 1990s, overfishing and poaching threatened *Huso*

huso, along with other sturgeon species prized for their roe, with extinction. "Everyone with a rowboat is out on the Caspian tossing sturgeon into the backs of their boats," a U.S. Customs agent told the *Los Angeles Times* in the late nineties.

In 1998, the Convention on International Trade in Endangered Species (CITES) started setting quotas on the harvesting of wild Caspian caviar. Some years, the amount deemed safe to take was none. In 2005, the U.S. Fish and Wildlife Service banned the importation of beluga, which had recently been added to the endangered species list. Beluga prices spiked, encouraging smugglers and imposters. The less beluga there was, the more "beluga" there was: some of it real, some of it fake, all of it illegal. A Warsaw police officer in charge of an anti-organized-crime unit was arrested at JFK with six accomplices and sixteen suitcases full of undeclared beluga, and special agents from U.S. Fish and Wildlife started to perform DNA tests on incoming caviar shipments, looking for fraud.

The restrictions on caviar have spawned a mini-industry of neologisms based on deep faith in the power of association. Label-imagery, Morris Kushner might have called it. "Beluga," which conjures visions of oligarchs, is the magic word. The largest caviar importer in America, Marky's, which is based in Miami, offers on its website "Prime B Dark Osetra Private Stock Caviar known as Beluga Type Caviar," which is about as meaningful as describing an African elephant as "Dark Gray Special Reserve Animal known as Lion Type Animal." The COO assured me that the company was going to revise its website soon. "This was written to indicate what others have called it," he said. "There is so much confusion."

One thing, at least, was clear. Before the ban, Marky's aquaculture branch brought fifty-five live *Huso huso* into the United States; when the fish mature in several years the company will have a federally enforced monopoly on beluga in the U.S. market. Another importer has registered the name River Beluga to refer to *Huso dauricus,* a sturgeon native to the Amur River, on the border of Russia and China. *Huso dauricus,* commonly known as kaluga, is a relative of beluga, but not a close one. One distributor I talked to, who deals in *Huso dauricus* raised on a farm in China, said that *his* importer invoices it to him as "beluga hybrid," which is how he represents it to the restaurants he supplies. "The beluga name is what consumers know, but there's no wild beluga on the market," he said. "You have people reaching out, saying, 'What's the next best thing?' You're paying for the scarcity of the species."

In 2000, when the embargo against Iran was loosened, Behroush Sharifi, an Iranian-born, English-educated, American Deadhead with a gigantic beard, decided to start importing from the Middle East. First it was carpets. Then he moved into botanicals: saffron, barberries, and manna from Iran; red hibiscus from Lebanon; mastic, a kind of ancient chewing gum, from Greece. Anointing himself the Saffron King, he trafficked in the ancient, storied, strange, and scarce. His customers were famous New York restaurants like Babbo, Daniel, Jean Georges, WD-50. Around the time he started his business, a friend at the Natural Resources Defense Council (NRDC) asked him for help. The group was petitioning Fish and Wildlife to add beluga to the endangered species list; the agency had missed a deadline to respond and now the NRDC could bring a lawsuit but needed a plaintiff. Sharifi had grown up spending summers on the Caspian, and had flirted with importing Iranian caviar. Helped by his testimony about the devastation of the fishery, beluga was added to the list, clearing the way for the 2005 ban. "Many foodies would be angry that I'd removed something so precious," he said.

In the absence of wild-caught Caspian caviar, a market for domestic roe, farmed and fished, has opened up. California has been producing caviar since the seventies, when the overthrow of the shah of Iran inspired fears—hopes?—of a shortage; now Petrossian carries it. Paddlefish eggs are coming out of the Ozarks; bowfin roe from the Atchafalaya Swamp gets exported to Moscow. (The FDA allows these products to be called caviar, but purists say that designation belongs only to sturgeon eggs.) On farms, delivery does not always mean death: some aqua-cultivators induce ovulation with synthetic oxytocin—Pitocin, which stimulates uterine contractions, is one—and then "milk" the fish, while others have experimented with cesarean sections. "It's not lost on me that a lovely unintended consequence of making caviar illegal is that it allows for this emergence, this wonderful domestic product," Sharifi told me. It is a product he has come to have a special feeling for, now that a new trade embargo has made importing saffron and other Iranian products illegal again. "Principles are one thing but you have to have bread in the bowl," he told me, explaining that he is now a seller of American caviar.

Ottolenghi's caviar, from a Mediterranean sturgeon called *Acipenser naccarii,* is raised sustainably on a farm in Grenada, and prepared according to a traditional Iranian recipe. I met

Philippe Barbier, the recipe master, in Spain: a French Basque with deep-set green eyes, a reddish beard, a yellow front tooth, and unlaced shoes. Driving through the countryside, he said that the culinary potential for farmed caviar was much greater than for the revered beluga, which no one dared serve other than with toast points and riced egg. The lower price of his stuff made it more like any other raw ingredient. "Chefs seem receptive—they're just looking for reassurance that it's a product no one will think they're silly for using," he said. Michel Trois-gros, the Michelin three-star chef at Maison Troisgros, in Paris, was using his caviar, he said, to make *payusnaya*, a paste that he formed into a thin sheet and wrapped around a soft-boiled quail egg. "When you cut it, all the yolk is coming out, like a little volcano!" he said. Troisgros had also filled the channels of cooked endive with the caviar and shaped them into black-and-white roses.

After Ottolenghi visited the farm with Barbier, he returned to Las Vegas determined to break into the room-service and private-jet menus of all the big casinos. Hopeful, he went to a major casino and presented the caviar to a team of chefs. They loved it; they especially loved the price. But then one of them asked if Ottolenghi could call it "beluga," as their current supplier was doing. "I told the exec chef what they were doing is illegal in front of 8 chefs and walked out," he wrote me in a text message. The next day, he wrote to me again, saying that he now had all the information he needed to show the casino that its caviar was illegally labeled. "So we should be able to get the business." If all else failed, he had put in a call to the authorities to get his competitor slapped.

. . .

Ottolenghi lives in a single-story stucco house he shares with his college roommate, Howie, who actually is a VIP host at Tao, the nightclub made famous by Tiger Woods and, with 1,400 covers on a peak night, one of the top-grossing restaurants in America. When I visited him in 2010, Ottolenghi was getting ready to open a small retail store, near the airport, where he hoped that chefs would shop on their days off. The living room was crowded with cans of Spanish olive oil, French green lentils, hand-kneaded fettuccine, specialty vinegar made by an ornery vintner in Napa, a huge bag of Szechuan peppercorns, and sixteen kinds of salt. In the kitchen cabinets, there were old balsamics and samples of water from all over the world, which Ottolenghi, researching for a special project, had tasted only after a twenty-four-hour fast. His fridge was full of awkward little pancakes of *payusnaya*, which, drawing on the Troisgros example, he was trying to interest his chefs in. Four long chest freezers full of bone-in hams and foie gras lobes lined the garage. A cream-colored 1951 Chevy panel truck, in which Sidney, the Artisanal Foods driver, makes deliveries, was parked out front.

Beside the front door was a small pond, which was home to three sturgeon—pets, Ottolenghi said, that also served as props. Several weeks before, he had bought a fish tank from a pet store, then called his domestic caviar supplier, in California, and asked if they could send him some sturgeon. He started going to chef meetings to pitch the Spanish caviar with one in tow. "He comes in with this fish tank sloshing water to show us what a sturgeon is," Alessandro Stratta told me. "I said, 'I know what a sturgeon is.' Next time, he'll come in here with a pig!" (Stratta placed an order.)

One morning, Ottolenghi went to the airport to pick up Helena Gonzalez, a beautiful twenty-seven-year-old Salvadoran woman whose parents started making foie gras in Sonoma, California, in the mid-eighties, and a better prop by a long shot than a sturgeon in a tank. Her foie gras was one of Ottolenghi's special products: it had the glow that comes from being obscenely delicious, extremely expensive (around $80 a pound), and soon to be unavailable. Foie gras, or "fatty liver," is made by *gavage,* force-feeding corn to ducks or geese until their livers swell to ten times their natural size. Animal-rights activists consider the feeding regimen to be torture, and in 2005 Arnold Schwarzenegger, who was at the time the governor of California, signed legislation to ban the sale and production of foie gras. Sonoma Artisan Foie Gras, the Gonzalezes' company, was the state's one producer. In deference to them, the bill was given a long sunset: they had until July 1, 2012, to invent a method of production that did not involve *gavage*, or close down. It was a rather hopeless proposition. Foie gras has been made the same way since the time of the Pharoahs.

Ottolenghi's first appointment with Gonzalez was at City Center, with Drew Terp, who was then the executive chef at barMASA and Shaboo, a pair of restaurants run by Masayoshi Takayama, whose flagship, Masa, is one of the most expensive restaurants in New York. Wearing a brown suit, a Bic behind his ear, and a pair of glasses tucked into the neckline of his shirt, and carrying a foam cooler loaded with duck breasts and foie gras, Ottolenghi led Gonzalez across the hectic, dimly lit casino floor and around a corner to a fifteen-foot-tall locked door. Beside the locked door was another door, which he tested and found open. He let himself in and sat down to wait for the chef. "It took me forever to find Masa," he said later. "I kept hearing about it. I was, like, 'There's a new really expensive restaurant? How am I not working with them?'"

Eventually, Terp appeared and took Ottolenghi and Gonzalez into the kitchen. "We use Hudson. That's what Chef Masa likes best," Terp, who is tall and fair, with full, rosy cheeks and a curl at his forehead, said. Hudson Valley Foie Gras, which is based in upstate New York, is the largest domestic producer of foie gras, and was Sonoma's primary competitor. "Chef Masa, when he finds something he likes, it's very difficult to get him to use other things." Ottolenghi extracted a big putty-colored lump from the cooler and handed it to Terp, who drew it close to his face and turned it over several times. Ottolenghi ventured that the feed used by Sonoma was, in his opinion, superior— cooked corn, with no added soy protein. Terp shaved off a tiny sliver of the lobe and pressed it into a pan with his index finger. It started to sizzle. "We go through five to six lobes a week," he said. "We do a five-hundred-dollar *omakase* menu, and I'll use half a lobe for a five-top."

Terp removed the piece of seared foie gras with a pair of chopsticks and set it on a cutting board. He tasted it; he liked it; price, he said, was no object. "I have to run it by Chef Masa," he said. "He's very demanding. I'll have to go through the whole lobe to make sure of the consistency." Ottolenghi asked if he could visit the following week, when the chef was in. "Sure,"

Terp said. "But it's just him tasting it and saying yes or no. No sales pitch, no talking about sustainability."

Sampling, Ottolenghi not only drops off tidbits but also collects them. The next day, at Andre's, at the Monte Carlo, an old-school fine-dining establishment with a grandfathered-in cigar lounge, custom Limoges china, and wine dating back to the French Revolution, Ottolenghi set to work on the chef, Gary FX LaMorte. Chef was an indoorsy-looking guy, with shiny dark hair. There was a lot Ottolenghi wanted to know: where he had worked before (another French restaurant), where his former colleague had gone (the Caribbean), where he got his rabbit. "I ask because rabbit really interests me," he said. "Rabbit doesn't require USDA approval to slaughter. Anyone can kill one and butcher it in their kitchen and sell it. One day I want to get into that." Picturing Ottolenghi's kitchen, with its view of an algae-covered swimming pool, I shivered. When they got around to the matter at hand, LaMorte mentioned that he needed duck fat for terrines. "We decant the clarified foie fat, chill the terrine, and brush the fat back on for a protective coating, just like you would do at your house in the 1880s or some shit," he said. "You can mix it with cocoa butter. It makes a great salad dressing."

"I want to see more dandelion being used," Ottolenghi said, making me wonder if he had a lead on a patch.

"I like it, but it makes you urinate a lot," LaMorte said.

For most of Las Vegas's history, food there broke down into three main categories: coffee shop, steak house, and buffet. For high rollers, there were gourmet rooms, with names like the

Sultan's Table and the House of Lords, where waiters in tuxedos plated Maine lobster and chateaubriand tableside. Restaurants were a way of fortifying gamblers, to keep them from straying too far from the tables and the slot machines.

The first big chef to come to Las Vegas was Wolfgang Puck, who had opened Spago, in Los Angeles, in the early eighties. The developer Sheldon Gordon approached him with the idea of putting a Spago in the Forum Shops at Caesars Palace, a mall that he planned to build in a parking lot where Formula One races had been held. Puck, who liked to go to Vegas for the fights and already had a branch of Spago in Tokyo, agreed, and the restaurant opened at the beginning of December 1992, when the only thing happening was the rodeo finals. "We had all these people come up to the open kitchen—they'd see the plates and think it was a buffet," Puck recalled. "I said, 'I didn't know they had so many cowboys here. I would've done a rib joint.'"

For the first several weeks, Puck thought he'd made a terrible mistake, and drank himself to sleep every night with a bottle of wine in front of the TV. Then New Year's came, the shows resumed, and the Consumer Electronics convention came to town. Spago had lines out the door. Steve Wynn started hanging out at the bar, and so did the Molaskys, big local developers. Puck would see customers from the L.A. Spago at the fights— Arnold Schwarzenegger, Jack Nicholson, Tony Danza—and bring them back to Spago afterward. Before long, the Vegas location was outperforming L.A.'s. "People started hearing the numbers we were doing at Spago," David Robins, the restaurant's chef, who moved to Las Vegas to help with the opening, told me. "I'd get calls saying, 'Did you really do a million this month?' I'd say, 'Actually, it was one-point-two.'"

In the late nineties, while getting ready to open the Bellagio, a $1.6-billion resort on the site of the old Dunes casino, Steve Wynn, mindful of Puck's success, decided that the property needed to be a dining destination. He sent a team of consultants out to recruit celebrity chefs, and when the Bellagio opened, in 1998, it housed world-class restaurants by Sirio Maccioni, Michael Mina, Julian Serrano, Todd English, and Jean-Georges Vongerichten. Soon every big casino had a roster of star chefs. Joël Robuchon came out of retirement to open two restaurants at the MGM Grand in 2005; in 2009, Pierre Gagnaire, a three-star Michelin chef in Paris, opened his first restaurant in the United States, at the Mandarin Oriental hotel at City Center.

From the beginning, the problem with haute cuisine in Las Vegas was ingredients. All you could get were frozen proteins and overstock produce. When Puck first arrived, he told me, "I went to visit a fish guy, who took me into a thirty-thousand-square-foot freezer. I said, 'No, no. That's not who we are. We want fresh tuna and salmon.'" He had his chefs drive a van to the Santa Monica Farmers Market for fruit and vegetables. As more and more high-level chefs arrived, a culture developed of what one chef called "FedEx cuisine." Claude Le Tohic, the executive chef at Robuchon, who won the 2010 James Beard Award for best chef in the Southwest, gets his butter and his cheese overnighted from France. According to Julian Serrano, it is easier to get good ingredients in Las Vegas than in San Francisco, where he used to work, because the airport there often gets fogged in, whereas in Las Vegas the weather is almost always clear, and a plane lands every three minutes at McCarran Field.

Paul Bartolotta, the chef at Bartolotta at Wynn, a complex that Steve Wynn opened in 2005, is perhaps the most extreme example. The concept of his restaurant—simple preparations of fish and crustaceans at exorbitant prices—depends on seafood being flown in as often as five times a week from the Mediterranean, in coolers equipped with microchips to monitor the temperature throughout the voyage. He has no patience with concerns about sustainability. "Las Vegas is a pilot project to see if man can live on the moon," he says. "There's nothing local— our water comes from somewhere else, our electricity comes from somewhere else." Fishermen have sent him texts in the middle of the night from their boats in the Adriatic, with pictures of themselves holding fresh-caught specimens and messages like "Want this fish?" On one such occasion, the fish was an eighteen-pound ombrina; when it arrived at the restaurant, forty-eight hours later, Bartolotta walked it onto the floor and offered it to a party of golfers as the main course in a tasting menu they had ordered. He took it back to the kitchen, sprinkled some salt and pepper on it, tied up the tail so it would fit in the oven, and within ninety minutes the golfers were eating it. Their bill came to nearly $5,000, before wine.

Another local feature is the wildly variable demand. Olivier Dubreuil, the executive chef at the Venetian and the Palazzo, which together command nearly two million square feet of convention space, says that he sometimes serves eighty thousand people one day and twenty thousand the next. "I can use five hundred *magrets* and then never use them again," he says. "I can use sixty pounds of foie gras in three days." Even in the age of cutbacks, the pharmaceutical companies still spend handsomely. When Tylenol comes to town, he told me, food budgets soar.

Vegas may be the one food town left in America where the ego of the customer still trumps the ego of the chef. If a big player wants a cheese pizza, he gets a cheese pizza, even at a formal French restaurant like Alex. I heard a story about a Korean high roller who travels twice a year to Wynn with an entourage of twenty-five and plays six-figure hands of baccarat. One night he tried Bartolotta and loved it so much that he arranged to bring his whole group back the following night. Only this time he was in the mood for a roast-beef dinner. So what did Bartolotta do? He went out and found some beef to roast. Bradley Ogden recently bought from Ottolenghi some 1890 balsamic vinegar in tiny bottles that looked as if they should hold perfume; they cost $350 apiece and would most likely be served to high rollers, after supper, on mother-of-pearl spoons. "Vegas is the entertainment capital of the world," David Robins, of Spago, says. "We want to treat customers with respect, and we want to take all their money."

A relative of mine who lived in Buffalo and went by the name Shorty Plumb used to run booze across the border to Canada in the back of a pickup truck loaded with horse manure, and never got caught. Truffle cheats follow that same rule of thumb: you hide the good stuff in with the shit. The sums of money involved can be vast. White truffles from Italy cost up to $4,500 a pound wholesale; black ones, $800. Claude Le Tohic,

Robuchon's executive chef, told me that when truffles are in season he goes through ten or twelve pounds of black ones and five pounds of white a week. He sometimes offers a six-course truffle tasting menu, which includes a truffle tart, and serves a truffle–foie dish topped with edible gold.

For an importer, the temptation to con can be strong. Some will stash a box of truffles deep inside a container load of something boring, like lettuce, to dodge the import tax. Others route their paperwork through places not within the bounds of the EU. For years, Ottolenghi says, all the European truffle companies were based in San Marino, a tiny independent republic in northern Italy, which was exempt; now most run their paperwork through Croatia. Another common trick, this one played on chefs, is to add a few worthless Chinese truffles to a box of black Italians; the color is indistinguishable, and the Chinese truffles take on the aroma of the more expensive ones. A chef would have to know the subtleties of truffle morphology to pick out the impostors, or isolate each truffle under a bell jar and smell it again after waiting fifteen minutes. Ottolenghi finds the chicanery infuriating; crooks serve as a good foil for virtue, but they make for tough competition in the marketplace. "Basically, selling truffles, you're a smuggler," he says.

I asked Joseph Magnano, the young, tattooed West Coast representative for Sabatino Tartufi, a large importer based in Umbria, about the business. At the time, he was the top truffle seller in Las Vegas, and he saw it as a magnet for come-latelies. "Every distributor in Las Vegas at one point or another will try to get in on it, try to get on my coattails," he said, agitated, between sales calls at the Wynn. He had on a black wool cap and carried a small cooler full of truffles. "But they don't know how to sell truffle. They don't *care* to know about truffle."

I asked if there was a lot of fraud. "Oh, a hundred percent," he said. "I'm not saying that *we* do it, but I'm saying it's there, especially during black winter–truffle season, because it's at the same time as Chinese truffle season. Chef will never know the difference if he doesn't know truffle. You *can* identify them, they have a different hardness, the flavor's different, they taste more rubbery, they're not as clean, the veins are skinnier, it's just not a good product. You can tell, if you know truffle." A Chinese truffle, Magnano said, smells like burned drip coffee, while a bad white truffle tastes like a greasy Lay's potato chip. But he dismissed Ottolenghi's priggishness. "It's not that the business has no ethics—it's a business," he said scornfully. "If you don't move product, you don't live."

A few years ago, Ottolenghi sent a letter to his chefs, announcing that, after twelve years, he was scaling down his truffle business, "because the only way to succeed selling truffles in Las Vegas is to have lower ethics and cheat more than your competitors." He went on to say that saffron, "a once noble spice," was going the same way, and claimed that not a single restaurant in Las Vegas was using pure product. Most of the saffron on the market—sold for $85 an ounce—was, he said, a hash of crocus parts dyed with red food coloring. He, on the other hand, was personally importing saffron directly from Spain. The letter served as an announcement that his fresh shipment had arrived and that he would be offering it for $145 an ounce.

While in Spain, Ottolenghi went to see Pina, his saffron source in La Mancha. "Saffron is the second product I started selling, after truffles," he told me. "Light products do well on the Internet." Pina has a lab where it analyzes competitors' saffron to suss out fakes, and Ottolenghi thought that this would be a selling point to chefs: they'd give him a one-gram sample of whatever they were using, he'd pay to have it tested at Pina, and if it turned out to be dyed the chefs would promise to buy from him. "I know I'm going to win that bet," he said.

After he got home, Ottolenghi was back on his beat, going from chef to chef, a brown leather satchel slung over his shoulder, hand-selling his goods: 100-percent-pure saffron; vanilla bean from Papua New Guinea; and a variety of salts, including one that had been smoked over a Chardonnay cask. It was 116 degrees, and, to his embarrassment, he couldn't wear a suit. Furthermore, his sturgeon had died, and Chef Robuchon had said no to the Spanish caviar. But SW Steakhouse had just ordered a kilo, for $1,500; barMASA was using the foie gras; and RM Seafood, Rick Moonen's sustainable fish restaurant at Mandalay Bay, had picked up both.

At midday, Ottolenghi trudged into the Rio, an old casino that houses the purchasing department for all the Harrah's properties in Las Vegas. He wound his way past giant carnival masks and fixated smokers staring at the slots, and through an unmarked door to the loading dock, where crates of plucked chickens sat next to plastic bags of precooked chili. In a windowless office off the dock, he sat down to make a pitch to a senior buyer. "I'm trying to convince everyone to switch to real saffron," Ottolenghi said. "It's terrible. There's more cheating going on in saffron than almost any other product." He pulled a jar from his satchel, and took off the top. A heady, tobacco-like aroma filled the room. He held up a piece, bright red, like a shrunken coral. "The fake ones, you put them in water, the water will turn orange-red from dye," he said. The buyer pushed a pair of glasses up onto his forehead. "Interesting," he said flatly. "Never knew that." Ottolenghi leaned in, and suggested that he could do a demonstration for the chefs, soaking the saffron from their stockrooms in water to show them what they really had: flavorless flower bits and food coloring. The buyer agreed, and Ottolenghi packed up his wares and said good-bye. But, rather than leaving, he started walking down the hall, popping his head into other buyers' offices, just to introduce himself and say hello and see if they might like to take a sniff of his vanilla from Papua New Guinea, which was the same species and just as good, based on his research, as the prized Tahitian stuff, and a bargain by comparison.

Ottolenghi has attended the Fancy Food Show since he was eight. (The minimum age is eighteen.) I went for the first time in 2012, to the winter show in San Francisco. Before long, I ran into Ruth Reichl, the former editor of *Gourmet* who had become the director of Gilt Taste, an ever-changing online market for everything from golden-roe bottarga to gluten-free pound cake. Reichl, an experienced showgoer, was reminiscing about weird, off-putting products past, like Gourm-Egg, a tube of extrudable hard-boiled eggs, for salad bars and restaurants. This time around, the novelties were throwbacks: "ancient grains," chia seeds, camote flour—subsistence fare from the early days of agriculture.

At Culinary Collective, a sophisticated Washington-based importer with a line of pre-Columbian flours and grains, Betsy Power was talking up *kañiwa*, a hearty, high-protein grain that grows in the Andean *altiplano,* which she had recently placed in some Whole Foods stores in Northern California. Power extolled *kañiwa*'s earthy, nutty flavor and its plumping ratio, comparing it favorably to its sometimes bitter-tasting cousin, quinoa. "People had started growing quinoa, due to the Western influence in the market," she said. "*Kañiwa* was out of favor. They were growing it for animals"—a sure sign that it was poised for exploitation by the wealthiest eaters. The rise of Bolivian quinoa, though, served as a warning: embraced by Americans as a high-brow carb, its price nearly tripled in five years, making it unaffordable to the poor Bolivians who once made it a staple of their diets but now relied on less-expensive processed foods.

"The caviar flows like glue at the show," Julia Child once joked. When an attractive Korean woman wearing a T-shirt that read "I'm Probiotic" walked by, I followed her back to her booth in search of something to eat. "Probiotics is the buzz-word," she said, spearing some red-hot kimchi on a toothpick and handing it to me. "The American palate is beginning to understand what live food means. Pasteurized and dead things are part of the old food system." Her card promised well-being to those who consumed "the Champagne of Pickles."

I found Stewart Reich, Max Ries's great-nephew, taking meetings on a tartan-covered café chair at the lavish Walkers Shortbread booth. Behind him, imposing wooden display cases were filled with cookie tins, down-lit like handbags at Hermès. Walkers was a success story—an obscure Scottish cookie discovered in the seventies by two guys from the Bronx as they traveled through Europe looking for products to import. They placed an order and figured that if the cookies didn't sell, they would give them away. At the time, Walkers was only in two or three countries; now it's a $200-million-a-year business, with a presence in eighty countries.

There were lots of things like that at the show: food givens that the old hands could trace back to their uncertain beginnings. "Balsamic vinegar is in everything now," Reich mused. "Not that long ago it was only available from Dean & DeLuca." Mario Foah, the panettone guy, had Reich beat on that; he later told me that he was one of the first to import it, in the early eighties, before anybody knew what it was. "I went to somebody's home in Milan and they made a risotto with balsamic vinegar. I said, 'What's *this* stuff?'" he recalled. He bottled it in a special straw-wrapped container, presented it at the Fancy Food Show, and dazzled the food press. "That was the year balsamic vinegar took off," he said.

At the next booth over were the remains of Reese, which Max Ries sold to Pet Milk in the mid-sixties. (He died at home on Lake Shore Drive in Chicago, in 1984.) Reese is currently owned by a distributors' consortium called World Finer Foods, which also represents Bonne Maman preserves, McCann's Irish Oatmeal, and Panda licorice. According to the consortium, Reese is still the country's top-selling brand of artichokes, water chestnuts, hearts of palm, and wine vinegar. The wall of Reese products looked like the contents of a mid-century bomb shelter: capers, anchovy fillets, asparagus spears, packed in glass and labeled with idealized pictures of the contents.

When I ran into Ottolenghi, he was wearing his blue blazer and khakis and had just come from a meeting in Seattle with some importers of *wagyu*, extra-fatty Japanese beef; a nearly three-year ban on imports, due to hoof-and-mouth, was soon to be lifted. After that, he had stopped at the Monterey Bay Aquarium to investigate the potential of selling sea urchins from the last sustainable population, off the coast of British Columbia. Here at the show he was excited about some vinegar made from rotten bananas. "I don't know who I'm going to sell it to—but someone!" he said. He spent a long time looking at the Cinco Jotas ham—an Ibérico even more expensive than Fermín, which was making its U.S. debut.

Then Ottolenghi saw something else, something slick and sleek and new, with a great story. It was Ian Purkayastha, a nineteen-year-old truffle merchant from Arkansas who had skipped college and was now the U.S. distributor for an esteemed Italian line, selling to Per Se, Daniel, and Jean Georges. (A few months later, he launched a new company, which specializes in wild edibles, like milkweed, pine bud, and Queen Anne's lace.) He was trim and confident, with heavy dark eyebrows, and was wearing what appeared to be an Armani suit. Ottolenghi checked him out, and offered his impartial assessment. Purkayastha was the genuine article. He said, "He's younger, and he sells *way* more truffles than I do."

PART II

DOWN THE
RABBIT HOLE

Four

THE
RAWESOME THREE

Neophilia and neophobia—loving and fearing the new—
are conflicting impulses that arise simultaneously in infants around the time that they attain mobility: babies
put everything in their mouths and start to reject the unfamiliar. That's about where I was with unusual food, the crawling
stage, when I heard about Rawesome, an expensive, all-cash,
members-only specialty store devoted to radically unprocessed
food, run out of a lot in Venice, California. Rawesome was
based on the topsy-turvy idea that "safe" food was food pro-
cured outside official channels. Its members strained the boundaries of food adventuring to the point of reckless abandon—and
did so with an attitude of extreme finickiness, in the name of
protecting their health.

Rawesome attracted a clientele of health-seekers, yoginis,
celebrities, and the seriously ill. The store, which advertised itself

with a sign that read "Rawesome Foods—Raw and Organic—Out of the Ordinary and Downright Extraordinary," carried provisions that were otherwise inaccessible: unheated honey from the Bolivian highlands (outside the fallout range of the A-bomb tests), sun-dried cashews from Bali, raw cow colostrum, goat whey, and camel milk from a dairy selling it for "craft use." Cheese came in unmarked tubs—often lacking dates or labels—and in the meat cooler there were jars containing raw bison kidneys, spleen, hearts, and testicles, which customers often sliced open and ate on the spot. "We had some real vampires going through there," a former Rawesome worker, who lived for a time in a shipping container on the lot, said. "Everyone wanted to suck the cow's udder." Liv Tyler and Mandy Moore shopped there occasionally. Mariel Hemingway was a regular, as were Peta Wilson and Vincent Gallo. Fred Segal, the boutique owner, ordered a box of food every week, and John Cusack's personal chef, Rawesome workers said, was forbidden to shop anywhere else.

James Stewart, Rawesome's owner, a robust man in his mid-sixties with a beachcomber's moustache and a wardrobe of Hawaiian shirts, had been in the food business a long time. As a teenager in the mid-sixties, Stewart told me, he moved from New York to California with his mother and sisters, who became famous Hollywood groupies; one of them, Reine, had a baby with Peter Tork of the Monkees. Stewart lived across from the Whiskey and got a job at HELP (Health, Education, Love, Peace), one of the city's first health-food stores, where he was introduced to the teachings of Yogi Bhajan, a Sikh who brought kundalini to the United States, and started wearing a turban.

He grew sprouts, which he sold to supermarkets, and worked for the Beach Boys at their store, Radiant Radish. One of Stewart's companies, an organic produce business, was called Green Energy. "I figured it was just green coming out of the ground, turning into money," he told me. "It was a cycle." For his ability to source shade-dried manuka raisins and dried persimmons—rarities in the seventies—he earned the nickname Mr. Exotic. By the time he opened Rawesome, he said, half the products he stocked could be found at regular health food stores and farmers' markets; the other half, the "unique products," he called them, were illegal.

Early one morning in the summer of 2011, as one of the coconut juicers—known around Rawesome for their stoned demeanor and their unsocialized way of wearing mud masks in public—started extracting the day's supply, there was a knock at the gate. Outside, more than a dozen agents from the FDA, the county health department, and the Franchise Tax Board had assembled, in raid jackets and tactical vests; armed LAPD officers provided security. Stewart was arrested and put in handcuffs. He had $9,000 in his pocket, because he'd been planning to go downtown to pick up merchandise. His fruit money was entered into evidence. Over the next several hours, a crowd of about a hundred Rawesome members gathered to watch as agents loaded produce onto a flatbed truck. When the agents dumped some eight hundred gallons of raw dairy down the kitchen drain, members wept.

At its core, Rawesome was a raw-milk business. For more than a year, it had been the subject of a nine-agency investigation, in which undercover agents infiltrated the network of dairy dealers supplying the club. Count 3, Overt Act 12 of the felony complaint for arrest warrant: "'Deb' is in beige colored Ford van. . . . When 'Customer Ward\Kennedy' asks for his order, 'Deb' searches through five ice coolers in the back of the van and pulls out the water-soaked order: six unlabeled containers of raw dairy products." The operatives, among them the feared California Department of Food and Agriculture investigator Scarlett Treviso—code-named La Rue—mingled with customers and, using what Stewart's lawyer said were "purse cams and pole cams," photographed Rawesome's cooler, dry-goods trailer, and open-air produce market. They also took pictures of members coming and going through a corrugated metal gate. What they saw there shocked them, including, according to the complaint, membership agreements that said, "'As a member, I completely reject and refuse all governmental standards . . . any governmental sanitation standards for food storage and display' and I am 'out of the jurisdiction of any governmental department and its regulations.'" An undercover source told me, "It was one of the two most extreme communities I've ever worked in. The other was animal rights."

The day of the bust, the police also went to Santa Paula, sixty miles away, to hit Healthy Family Farms, a small operation that supplied the club with poultry, eggs, and, for a time, raw goat products from a forty-head herd that Rawesome boarded there. The farmer, Sharon Palmer, a single parent who manages the farm with her three teenagers, was arrested. A fifty-nine-year-old graphic designer named Eugenie Victoria Bloch, a Rawesome member who helped sell Palmer's products

at farmers' markets, was also arrested, outside her home in Los
Angeles.

Stewart, Palmer, and Bloch, who came to be known as the
Rawesome Three, were charged with felony counts of conspir-
acy; Stewart and Palmer were charged with an additional two
felonies, for running an unlicensed milk plant and processing
milk products without pasteurization, and with various misdemeanors, including counts of poor sanitation and improper
labeling. (All three pleaded not guilty to all the charges.) The
the tax-board data indicated that Rawesome was generating
more than $500,000 a year in income, yet neither the business
nor the proprietor had filed state tax returns. Stewart's bail was
set at $123,000, with the stipulation, common in drug cases,
that he be held until the court could ascertain that the bail was
not "feloniously obtained"—high stakes for a grocer. For his
defense, he hired Ajna Sharma-Wilson, at the time an attorney
at one of the top marijuana-defense firms in Los Angeles. The
analogy was plain: raw milk was the new pot, only harder to get.

Paranoia and defiance rippled through the Rawesome community after the raid. At a screening of *Farmageddon*, a documentary about small producers victimized by national and state
food-safety laws, which concludes with absurd footage of an
earlier raid on Rawesome, in 2010—agents, guns drawn, stalk-
ing among crates of fruits and vegetables—Stewart, in a white
palm-tree shirt unbuttoned to his sternum, said that he was not
at liberty to talk about some of what he had learned from the
discovery. A big, mustachioed man, hunkered down in his chair,
cautioned him to be even more circumspect. In a thick accent,

he said, "Are you aware that there is possibly an informer sitting amongst us right now?"

Sharma-Wilson tossed her long dark hair. "I invite an informer to hear this," she said. "Our forefathers drank straight from a cow." She went on, "This is a guerilla war. This all started with the Pure Food and Drugs Act of 1906. The FDA actually stated recently that 'There is no "deeply rooted" historical tradition of unfettered access to foods of all kinds.'"

At a hearing in October 2011, thirty supporters wearing white T-shirts that read "Raw Milk Heals" gathered outside the courtroom. Many were baffled by what had befallen their neighborhood market. "Rawesome was an intelligent local food ecosystem. It was alive, and it was regulating itself on a level so far beyond what the USDA or the FDA means when it says 'food safety,'" Camilla Griggers, who teaches English at a nearby college, said. "That we would be dragged through the court system on a food-safety issue is so laughable. Rawesome was a gourmet club par excellence of the best food you could get anywhere in the world."

Never mind the immersion circulators and the hydrocolloids, refined American cuisine has a regressive side, wrapped up in nostalgia for an idealized past. Raw milk stirs the hedonism of food lovers in a special way. After relying for years on milk smuggled from California and Utah, Ottolenghi, in Las Vegas, is trying to build Nevada's first raw-milk dairy. Because raw milk is not heated or homogenized and often comes from animals raised on pasture, it tends to be richer and sweeter and, sometimes, to retain a whiff of the farm—the slightly discom-fiting flavor known to connoisseurs as "cow butt." To chefs, it is almost mystical. "Pasteurization strips away layers of complexity, layers of aromatics," Daniel Patterson, who has used raw milk to make custard and eggless ice cream at Coi, his two-Michelin-star restaurant in San Francisco, said. "At the beginning of spring, the milk is at its sweetest. The cows are getting a lot of herbs that are really verdant and green, and the milk has a higher fat content." It is not just the flavor, though, it's what it represents: something unprocessed, sentimental, pure. "Raw milk is a primary touchstone of that sort of agrarian, old-fashioned way of life," Patterson said.

Another highly regarded California chef told me he had helped a nearby farmer buy three cows from a breed carefully picked for the character of its milk and set up a small herd share, an agreement of uncertain legality whereby consumers own a percentage of a herd and are entitled to an allotment of milk. The farmer insisted on cash payments, no paper trail. "Only recently have they allowed receipts to go through my book-keeper, but even now we don't say what it's for," the chef told me. "We say 'cow services.'" He uses the raw cream to make butter, ice cream, and a *cajeta*—Mexican caramel—that he des-cribes as "haunting." He said, "Dairy is the single most delicate and sensitive indicator of *terroir* I have encountered. When you take milk or cream and pasteurize it and homogenize it, you've killed the originality."

Naturally, I wanted to try it. When I went to the chef's res-taurant, though, I thought it wise to pass the butter up. I had just found out that I was pregnant. Milk, being rich in protein and low in acid, is one of the best growth mediums on the planet. Bacteria love it. Unpasteurized milk can carry salmonella, campylobacter, and *E. coli* O157:H7, the strain that came to public attention in the nineties, when four children died after eating contaminated meat at Jack in the Box. Listeria—which can cause miscarriage, premature birth, and newborn death—has been traced to *queso fresco*–style raw-milk cheeses, sometimes known as "bathtub cheese," a reference to unsanitary home-production methods. The USDA fact sheet for consumers that I found online offered unambiguous advice. If you want to avoid listeriosis, it said, "Do not drink raw (unpasteurized) milk."

Only a small fraction of the population—between 1 and 3 percent—drinks raw milk, and fewer than 200 cases of outbreak-related foodborne illness are attributed to it each year. Still, its popularity is rising, and regulators, puzzled by the raw-milk phenomenon, are growing concerned. A recent CDC study reported that raw dairy was 150 times more likely than pasteurized to cause an outbreak. Tanya Roberts, a retired risk assessor for the USDA who specializes in *E. coli* O157:H7, told me, "I would never drink it. It's *loaded* with pathogens!" The FDA "strongly advises against the consumption of raw milk," maintaining that there is no nutritional advantage and a great health risk; John Sheehan, the agency's director of dairy food safety, has likened it to "playing Russian roulette with your health."

The government's real objection to raw milk is that they think people are playing Russian roulette with their *children's* health. Pasteurization was introduced to the American dairy industry to solve a children's-health crisis. By the mid-nineteenth century, most of the milk available in cities was supplied by "swill dairies," stables built alongside distilleries, where cows were fed macerated grain left over from the production of whiskey. The spent grains boosted milk production temporarily but left the cows—confined to dirty, crowded pens—malnourished and prone to disease. In 1858, *The New York Times* published an editorial titled "How We Poison Our Children," decrying the "bluish, white compound of true milk, pus and dirty water" and blaming swill milk for eight thousand infant deaths in the city the previous year. "The article which had borne from the beginning of the world a reputation for wholesomeness was in reality a deadly poison," the *Times* said. The state of milk was "intolerable to civilized society."

Four years later, Louis Pasteur came up with a heat treatment to kill bacteria in wine, and his method was soon applied to milk. When Nathan Straus, a philanthropist and later a co-owner of Macy's, set up depots where poor families could get pasteurized milk at discounted prices, the number of deaths among New York City babies dropped precipitously. What began as an argument for treating milk produced under unsanitary conditions became an argument for treating all milk. Speaking at the Pasteur Institute in 1905, the director of the depots read a statement from Straus saying, "It is milk—raw milk, diseased milk—which is responsible for the largest percentage of sickness in the world. . . . I hold that the only safe rule is—Pasteurize the entire milk supply and make it a function of the municipality."

Others, believing that pasteurization should only be a last resort, argued for dairies to be inspected rigorously and held to strict hygienic standards. Though a number of states set up "medical milk commissions" to oversee a dairy certification process, pasteurization, the more efficient and fool-proof approach, won out. Raw-milk sales are now illegal in eleven states and permitted in a number of others exclusively through herd-share agreements and on-farm sales; in four states, raw milk can be sold only as pet food.

Since 1987, when Ralph Nader's Public Citizen organization sued the Department of Health and Human Services to prohibit interstate commerce in raw milk, it has been a crime to transport it for sale across state lines. The resulting underground market is by definition unregulated; consumers must take it on faith that the milk is clean, something that, without testing, even the farmer can't know for sure. Good standards for inspection and proper labeling could significantly reduce the likelihood of outbreaks, but for now the two sides—those who call for unfettered access and those who completely oppose it—are deadlocked. "The conversation needs to start with really solid facts about the incidence of bacteria in raw milk," Jo Robinson, an investigative journalist who runs the website Eat Wild, says. "We're not doing enough to reduce those risks."

More than a hundred years ago, Ukrainian scientist Elie Metchnikoff, who was the deputy director at the Pasteur Institute laboratory in Paris, identified the health benefits of bacteria associated with fermentation. (He won the Nobel Prize and is considered the founder of the field of probiotics.) Rawesome extended this idea to all bacteria, claiming that a disease-resistant gut must be populated with the kinds of microorganisms most people strenuously avoid. In order to shop there, you had to sign an agreement saying that you preferred your food to "contain microbes, including but not limited to salmonella, E. coli, campylobacter, listeria, gangrene and parasites" and liked your eggs "completely unrefrigerated and unwashed from the chicken and covered with bacteria and poultry feces." Members not only rejected government food-safety standards as inapplicable to their nutritional requirements; they found them to be dangerous, because they allow for food to be treated with radiation and antibacterial chemicals. In the 2010 raid on Rawesome, the California Department of Food and Agriculture took samples of cheese made by a dairy in Missouri and found that they tested positive for trace amounts of listeria. "We told them we threw it out, but I don't think we did," a former USDA employee who worked at Rawesome for two years told me. "Listeria really didn't matter."

Suspicion of technology runs deep in the raw-milk movement. In the 1930s, a Cleveland dentist named Weston A. Price traveled around the world studying isolated populations experiencing their first exposure to "the displacing foods of modern commerce." In *Nutrition and Physical Degeneration*, which has become a central text for the movement, he wrote that people who ate unprocessed, indigenous foods had strong teeth, regular bone structure, and overall good health, whereas those who had adopted an American diet—refined sugar, white flour, pasteurized and skim milk, and hydrogenated oils—had cavities, facial deformities, and other problems, which they passed along to their children.

Advocates of raw milk hold that pasteurization kills enzymes that make food digestible and bacteria that contribute to a healthy immune system. Drinking raw milk, they say, confers numerous health benefits—vitality, digestive vigor, strong teeth, clear skin—and even has the power to treat serious ailments, such as diabetes, cancer, and autism. Sally Fallon Morell, the founder of an advocacy group informed by Price's work, recommends feeding raw milk to infants. (A pamphlet from her organization entitled "Homemade Raw Milk Formula for Babies, and Raw Milk for Toddlers & Children," equates breast milk with unpasteurized cow's milk, claiming that both contain "active biological systems that naturally protect the milk itself—and the infant who drinks it—from infection.") Carola Caldwell, a registered nurse who drove several hours from Lake Arrowhead to shop at Rawesome, overrode years of medical training to feed her son raw milk and meat. She told me that the diet had cured him of extreme allergies, chemical sensitivity, and moodiness. "Within three weeks of starting raw food, he became a different child," she said.

There has been little science to support these claims. The closest thing to an objective body of data appeared in 2011, with the publication of a large-sample study linking children's consumption of unheated "farm milk" to reduced rates of asthma and allergies. The researchers, based in Europe, where raw milk is more widely accepted, determined that whey protein was the protective element, but they stopped short of advising people to consume raw milk, because of the risk of pathogens. The next step, they wrote, would be to develop "ways of processing and preserving a safe and preventive milk."

· · ·

Raw milk has always been legal in California, but the preponderance of regulation has made it hard to come by. In the late nineties, not long after James Stewart started selling raw milk, the state's largest provider shut down its raw operation, leaving, by Stewart's count, eight licensed raw-milk cows. As he searched for new supplies, he heard from Mark McAfee, a former paramedic who had inherited his grandparents' farm, in Fresno. "I called up James and said, 'I've got two hundred and fifty cows here, all certified organic or on grass,'" McAfee told me. "He says, 'I'll be there in three hours.'" According to McAfee, Stewart singlehandedly rebuilt the market for raw milk in Southern California, and introduced him to the nutritionist Aajonus Vonderplanitz, a former *General Hospital* actor who claims to have cured himself of multiple cancers by eating a diet of raw meat, eggs, and milk, and sharply restricting his water intake. Vonderplanitz, who calls his approach the Primal Diet, says that for a treat he bleeds meat into raw milk: "Tastes like ice cream!" Vonderplanitz became an investor in the farm, and his followers became McAfee's customers. Organic Pastures is now, by McAfee's estimation, the largest raw dairy in the world, with 430 cows. It produces 2,400 gallons of milk a day, which retails for $16 a gallon.

One chilly November day, I drove out to Organic Pastures with McAfee, an energetic, trim man who was wearing a thick parka and clean blue jeans. The first time I had seen him, at a rally before one of Stewart's court appearances, he was drawing battle lines from a podium. "Look at the frickin' enemy. Remember who they are: Monsanto, Tyson, Cargill, the FDA," he said into a microphone. "In ignorance, our great-grandparents traded freedom for safety."

Now, in the car, McAfee continued his narrative of struggle. "When people start drinking raw milk, it's like this awakening," he said. "It's a phenomenally transforming immune-system food that is largely oppressed, suppressed, ignored, vilified, hated by processors and those that are involved with the structure of the American Dairy Association," he said. "It's a massive food fight."

That day, McAfee was waiting for the state to lift a month-long embargo on his milk. For the second time in five years, Organic Pastures had been implicated in an outbreak of *E. coli* O157:H7. Five young children had fallen ill; three were hospitalized and treated for hemolytic uremic syndrome, which can lead to kidney failure. The same strain had been found in his calving pen, and he had instituted new safety procedures at the farm. Still, the embargo was costing him $150,000 a week, and he felt that the state was punishing him intentionally. The recall had driven the price of raw milk in some stores up to $40 a gallon, with priority going to mothers. "We've been trying to keep the peace with all of our consumers," he told me.

McAfee pulled into the farm and stopped beside a village of neat trailers: an office, a retail store, and a creamery, where hundreds of bottles stood waiting to be sent out. He talked with a manager, and said grimly, "It looks like we won't be getting released today." We drove down an unpaved road, past McAfee's house, a large Mediterranean spread with a pool, a pair of pet goats, and a hangar where he keeps a plane. In the dairy barn, a row of cows with steaming, swollen undercarriages lined up to be milked. Workers hosed them down—manure is a major potential source of pathogens—then stripped their teats with iodine. The state requires frequent testing, and McAfee takes expensive precautions to keep the milk clean. But, he said, "Manure is the carrier of the beneficial bacteria found in raw milk. The whole pasteurization community does not understand that at all."

Most milk on the market comes from animals fed a diet containing corn and soy—typically genetically modified—rather than grass, the food they evolved to digest. Since 2004, milk has been legally identified as an allergen; the FDA and the CDC both cite it first, before shellfish, nuts, and wheat, on their lists of top allergens. Perhaps as a consequence, in recent years people have been drinking less of it, instead choosing alternatives like soy, almond, and rice milk. At the same time, prices for feed and fuel have escalated, and many dairies have gone out of business. There has been a spate of dairyman suicides, several of them in California. But, since McAfee's previous *E. coli* recall, in 2006, when six children got sick after drinking his products, Organic Pastures has grown steadily. McAfee is doing far better than most of his pasteurizing counterparts; the company, he says, sold $9.6 million worth of milk products in 2012.

One winter morning, with a heavy fog lying over Los Angeles, the Dairy Fairy, a Rawesome member who quietly assumed Stewart's procurement responsibilities after the bust, got in her car and headed for the drop. Every week, she takes orders from the Rawesome diaspora for raw dairy, sauerkraut, and meat, most of it transported from Amish country in truck space rented from a large produce operation. To compensate her for her time, she is given a box of groceries, which is meaningful, since she works freelance, and she and her boyfriend spend about $500 a week on food. (Their dog eats raw, too.)

At first, the drop had gone down in public parks across the city, but the Dairy Fairy had decided that was too risky. One day, at a convenience store, she noticed a man selling cars off the lot. "I was like, That's kind of shady," she said. "So I went and talked to the owner. He said, 'I'm from Egypt—I love raw milk!' I trade him milk for us to park our truck here." The beauty of the location, she said, is that trucks come and go all day long; no one notices the milk truck, unmarked and inconspicuous, parked in a corner of the lot.

The truck was waiting when she arrived. A young couple popped out of the cab; the woman had a pixie cut and was wearing knee-high yellow-and-black athletic socks from a CrossFit gym. The man helped the Dairy Fairy unload from her trunk two cases of black-market raw butter, made with cream from a nonfat-yogurt operation in New England, priced at $16 a pound. "This stuff is sacred!" the Dairy Fairy said. The butter-maker, she said, demanded that they rendezvous in strange spots to make the handoff: cash up front for butter. The last time, it had been at LAX. This time, she had had to meet him by the side of the road in Pasadena.

As the sun burned through the fog, the former members of Rawesome started to arrive: skinny women on bicycles, old ladies with tote bags, a CPA in a shiny black BMW SUV. Vincent

Gallo—pink sunglasses, lumberjack shirt, moccasins—came for his box, which included goat yogurt made by someone who used to work at Rawesome. "I go up in the mountains and get the raw goat milk," the yogurt-maker said. "I actually have to sign a waiver saying I won't bring anyone up there or say who they are. They are top secret." Business was good, he said. "I'm selling a *ton* of colostrum."

An attractive woman with flowing hair opened her box and drank from a quart of milk. "I love how the eggs were so full of poo last week," she said, with a thick milk moustache. "I got some really poocy ones and I was like, Yeah!" Eating this way, she told me later, made her feel free—liberated from the oppression of modern life, especially that of refrigeration—though it hampered her in certain ways, too. Restaurant meals were impossible: she had to bring her own raw ground bison meat, which she wrapped in prosciutto and smeared with raw butter she carried with her in a mason jar. She just had one thing to tell me: she hoped I wasn't eating yogurt from the grocery store. "That stuff is *so* bad for you," she said.

A few weeks later, the Dairy Fairy called me. She'd had an uncomfortable conversation with the butter-maker, who runs a successful gourmet business and sees no advantage in exposing his dealings in contraband dairy. "He said, 'You were the drug dealer! The drug dealer does not talk to the media!'"

To many in the national food-freedom movement, raw milk is the test case. Two years ago, the Farm-to-Consumer Legal Defense Fund, a nonprofit legal organization that helps raw-milk farmers, sued the FDA to lift the ban on interstate sales. (The suit was dismissed.) In responding, the FDA asserted, "There is no absolute right to consume or feed children any particular food." Statements like this stoke anxiety about the government's intentions. "Raw milk is just symbolic of this attitude of government regulators that they are the ones that make the decisions about what foods we can have," David Gumpert, an advocate-journalist who writes a blog called *The Complete Patient*, says. "You have this trend now toward irradiation. It's not required, but it's been sanctioned by the FDA. The next step may be for the FDA to require that all spinach *has* to be irradiated."

In recent years, the FDA has raided Amish and Mennonite farms that supply unpasteurized dairy products to out-of-state food clubs; in 2011, a farmer in Pennsylvania was driven out of business. The raid at Rawesome appeared to be an escalation of a strategy that raw-milkers think aims to kill the business entirely. Mike Adams, the editor of the website Natural News, compared undercover regulating agents to the East German Stasi, and warned of reprisals. "I believe we are very close to entering the age of a shooting war between farmers and the F.D.A.," he wrote. "I would encourage the F.D.A. agents who are no doubt reading this to strongly consider: Is your war against raw milk worth risking your life?"

"How far down the rabbit hole do you want to go?" Ajna Sharma-Wilson, the lawyer, asked me. Several months after the raid, she and Stewart and a group of his supporters converged at a hotel in Las Vegas, to attend the Constitutional Sheriffs and Peace Officers Association convention, an event put on by Richard Mack, a former sheriff from Arizona who successfully challenged a provision of the Brady Bill before the Supreme Court and was running for Congress as a Republican from Texas. I met them there. Mack, who told me that he'd spoken at "more Tea Party events than Sarah Palin," had drawn a hundred sheriffs, from across the country, who feel that the federal government is infringing on individual rights. He had invited the raw-milkers, he told me, because he wanted to educate both the sheriffs and the lawbreakers. "I want them to call their sheriff," he said. "I want their sheriff to protect them from the FDA."

Among the booths—Gun Owners of America, the John Birch Society, anti-income-tax proponents selling a CD called *The Politics of Jesus*—was a table piled with raw cheeses and fresh produce. The vegetables had come from a sustainable Nevada farm that had recently become a food-freedom darling when a health inspector showed up at a "farm to table" dinner and made the farmer pour bleach on the vegetables, maintaining that, because she could not determine how long ago they had been cut, they were unfit even for pigs.

At the table were several Raw Milk Freedom Riders, mothers who practice civil disobedience by crossing state lines with raw milk. Their splashiest protest so far has been a raw-milk-and-cookie sit-in on the steps of the FDA, in Silver Spring, Maryland. One of them had a seven-month-old baby on her hip. Sheriff Mack, an imposing figure in cowboy boots, a turquoise shirt, and a loosened teal-colored tie, kept throwing his arm around her and joking that he was going to arrest her for feeding her baby unpasteurized breast milk.

The mother was around my age and lived outside Washington, D.C.; she had started drinking raw milk when pregnant with her second baby. (This one was her fifth.) I asked her if she wanted to walk around and check out the booths. I kept looking for signs of the culture clash between the raw-milkers and the antigovernment extremists, but I couldn't get purchase. The raw-milkers claimed to be on board with everything, from putting a stop to roadside sobriety tests to ending seat-belt laws. Apparently, wanting the government out of their food colored everything for them.

Aside from the Freedom Riders' farm table, the only other food booth belonged to Freeze Dry Guy, a company that sells "freeze-dried foods for uncertainties." Preppers, as the community of apocalypse-ready food-hoarders is known, take food self-sufficiency to an extreme. Freeze Dry Guy's pitch was Store What You Eat—the idea being that if you're a big meat-eater, you're not going to want to add adjusting to a vegan diet to your list of problems when catastrophe strikes. Germans starved after World War II, the marketing material said, because they considered corn to be pig food. "These were not stupid people. They just had strong prejudices about what they would not eat. . . . Ever had monkey's brains, goat's eyes or grubs? Ever try to make an 18 month old child eat Brussels sprouts? Good luck! What if that were all you had?"

The Freedom Rider stared at a huge can of freeze-dried "Oriental-style spicy chicken": monkey's brains to her. Finally, a wedge issue! "Wow," she said, as she read down the list of industrial and GMO ingredients. "Wow."

At lunchtime, a buffet was set up in the middle of the room, with cold cuts, pasta salad, and bags of chips. Sheriff Mack loaded up a plate. "I grew up absolutely hating milk," he told me.

"I would gag on it! Now when I drink their milk, maybe it tastes better to me because it's freedom milk. It just has a little rebellious flavor in it. To me, it's the new civil rights. It's Rosa Parks."

Mack wandered over to the farm booth and asked one of the women there if she had eaten. "We brought our food, 'cause this is genetically modified," she said, pointing at the bag of popcorn in his hand. Someone poured Mack a glass of milk, and he turned to face the roomful of sheriffs—old fellows, mostly, with holstered handguns at their hips. The raw-milkers cheered as Mack took a big, showy sip and called out, "Freedom milk! Freedom milk!"

That night, Stewart's supporters threw an "ice-cream speakeasy" for the sheriffs in one of the hotel rooms. There was uncured sausage and raw cheese made by an Amish farmer currently fighting charges in Wisconsin. The raw milk was flowing, as was the cold-pressed hibiscus juice, sweetened with raw honey.

"I heard you won't touch anything raw," a goat farmer from Utah said, looking at me pityingly. In a small seating area, Stewart arranged tangerines, carob pods, and Satsuma mandarins on platters. Along one wall was a giant freezer filled with raw-milk ice cream: cherry from the Dairy Fairy, and chocolate and vanilla that Sharma-Wilson and the woman who loved dirty eggs had made in their hotel room that afternoon. "I sniffed every egg," the woman said, meaning to reassure.

The romance of the small farmer is a powerful thing in the American food marketplace. The reality can be jarring. Sharon Palmer, who had taken up farming after a career in business, sought to connect Healthy Family Farms to this story, describing it as a "sustainable, pasture-based farm," where all the animals—chickens, ducks, Cornish game hens, lambs, cows, milk-fed pigs—are raised from birth and harvested by hand. When she was arrested in August 2011, she again positioned herself as part of a larger narrative, telling the *Ventura County Star*, "It's not just about me. It's happening all over the country. I am very, very hopeful that this will become apparent that this is government abuse."

But just because a farm is small does not mean that the farmer always makes good decisions about how he raises the food you eat. A community that resists labeling and inspection as government intrusion puts itself at the mercy of its suppliers. (One longtime customer complained to me of buying rancid pork from Rawesome in an undated package, but he also used the occasion to brag that his gut microflora were strong enough to handle it.) Although Rawesome is held up by those who mourn it as a paradigm of intimate, enlightened consumership, its members may have known less about the origins of their food than they thought. A few years ago, a splinter group led by Aajonus Vonderplanitz began to question the integrity of Healthy Family Farms, claiming that the chicken and the eggs were outsourced and contained high levels of mercury and sodium. (Palmer and Stewart admitted to briefly selling eggs from another farm, but dispute the lab tests.) The former USDA employee who worked at Rawesome said that she was furious to discover that the chickens she believed to be exclusively pasture-fed were in fact finished on corn. "There's no such thing as non-GMO corn feed!" she said.

From the Dairy Fairy, I bought a pound of sacred butter and some milk in a plain, lightly sweating plastic gallon jug—no date, no label. It was yellowish, with a thick mantle of cream. I was tempted, but I didn't dare. It came all the way from Pennsylvania, and, visions of Amish country notwithstanding, I had no clue what that farm looked like. I poured my husband a glass. "It coats your mouth, almost like drinking half-and-half," he said, pronouncing it delicious. Five minutes later, he said the taste was still with him: a gamey, sweet-hay-manure flavor that intensified when he stepped outside.

The butter stayed in the fridge until I got word of a Primal Diet potluck hosted by Vonderplanitz at a condominium in Marina del Rey. Etiquette required that I bring something from Vonderplanitz's recipe book—"Nuts over Meat" (raw lamb on a pile of zucchini, covered in fresh nut butter), say, or a flask of "Power Drink" (raw liver, thyroid, testis or ovary, lung, brain, adrenal gland; raw milk; red onions). I took the butter instead, placing it on the counter in the kitchen, next to room-temperature oysters, raw chicken chunks, strips of raw red bison, cut fruit bobbing in cream, and a few open jars of raw milk. The whole room stank: warm, bilious, inescapably animal, like a nursery full of neglected babies surrounded by panting carnivores.

Vonderplanitz sat on a deep couch, among leopard-print pillows and faux-fur throws, surrounded by three young acolytes. Double-height windows looked out on the beach. He told me about his clients who thrived on raw food during their pregnancies. "It's so good for your baby," he said, and invited me to eat. "You have to pick it up by your hand, real primitive, cannibal-like," he said, widening his pale blue eyes and smiling to show his strong teeth. "Thank you," I said, but didn't move from the couch. He introduced me to his friends, two heavy-browed body-building brothers in their twenties and the nineteen-year-old girlfriend of one of them, who was a personal trainer. They told me that, on Vonderplanitz's recommendation, they had started eating rotting meat, though it was sometimes hard to do. "When the beef is green, you're like, 'Uhhhhhh,'" the young woman said. "My dad was pissed, like, 'What are you doing? You're going to be sick.'"

Vonderplanitz specifies using the highest-quality meat, and the young folk complained of the expense. The older brother said that when he couldn't afford gourmet meat, he ate spoiled meat from the regular supermarket. I let that sink in for a second: these middle-class kids were deliberately eating like the survivors of an apocalypse. It seemed to me they'd cherry-picked a losing combination, though—the modern convenience of cheap conventional beef with the caveman's limitation of eating it raw.

"What could be healthier than eating something completely unprocessed?" the older brother said.

"Like the cavemen did," the young woman said.

"Animals don't cook their food. They can survive anything. Humans on a cooked diet are weaker."

Vonderplanitz turned to me. He was bothered by the fact that I hadn't helped myself to the buffet. "Are you in any way connected with any government agency?" he asked. I reassured him, breathing through my mouth, that I was not, and got out of there before I embarrassed myself by throwing up all over the faux fur.

.   .   .

Not long after that, I had a dream the egg lady asked me how much grocery-store yogurt I was eating and I lied. I was sick of people telling me what to eat and what not to eat; I had come to my own conclusion about it and wanted to be left alone. In my irritation, I began to appreciate how maddening it must be for someone who believes that raw milk is saving her own or her child's life to be told she can't have it. Imagine if the annoying people interfering with the very private decision of what I ought to eat to stay healthy represented the federal government. No wonder the raw-milkers took refuge in the suffocating, self-enclosed world of the like-minded. It felt safe to them.

In the end, the Rawesome Three never went to trial for their alleged milk crimes. Stewart, who had spent time in jail on a related matter after failing to make bail, pleaded guilty to two misdemeanors, for processing raw goat milk at Healthy Family Farms and for operating a food facility—the Rawesome lot—without a permit; he was sentenced to 253 days in county jail, but credited for time served. In a separate case, he also pleaded guilty to two counts of felony tax evasion, and was given a suspended sentence of sixteen months in jail, and required to pay some $325,000 in restitution to the Franchise Tax Board. Palmer pleaded to a single misdemeanor, for having her dairy in an "insanitary condition" on the day of the raid. She had to pay a fine and perform forty hours of community service. Bloch, who took a misdemeanor for improperly labeling food, paid a hundred-dollar fine. All the rest of the charges were dismissed.

You can buy raw meat at the grocery store and feed it to

your kids and no one can stop you. But milk has exceptional emotional power. Be it human or cow, it is the first food to which we are exposed, making it unlike other products, both for consumers, who associate it with basic nourishment, and for regulators, who see its oversight as a grave responsibility. Michele Jay-Russell, of the Western Institute for Food Safety & Security at U.C. Davis, told me, "From a public-health perspective, milk has fallen into the category of water. Providing a clean milk and water supply is fundamental to what the government sees as its job." But she acknowledges the frustration of consumers who can't get a product that they feel they need. "The crux of the conundrum is: Why shouldn't it be their choice?"

Five

DOUBLE DARE

The Food and Drug Administration was the great achievement of the pure-food movement, and a centerpiece of Progressive Era reform. Harvey W. Wiley, known in bureaucratic history as the Father of the FDA, started his career in Washington in 1883, as chief chemist at the Department of Agriculture, which at that time was tasked not with meat inspection but with boosting the country's agricultural output. His office was founded to verify the uniqueness of fertilizer formulas for those seeking patents. Six feet tall, and more than two hundred pounds, with, a biographer noted, "only a suggestion of a paunch to testify to his fondness for the pleasures of the table," Wiley was an outspoken and controversial crusader for unadulterated, properly labeled food.

Unlike today, when diners seek adventure, eating in the nineteenth century, especially for the poor, was an act of inadvertent daring. Rapid urbanization had cut people off from the sources of their food; mass production was changing that food's very character. Refrigeration was limited. Chicanery and fraud were common. Unscrupulous and ignorant producers, trying to stretch shelf life or save on ingredients, put ashes in bread and formaldehyde in milk; chemical preservatives like borax, a laundry booster, were routinely added to perishable foods to mask or defer spoilage.

Born in a log cabin in Indiana to a family that grew almost all their own food and traded milk and butter for whatever they could not make themselves, Wiley lamented the industrialization of the food system. "In the good old days preceding and immediately following the War between the States, there was little need of protection of the people from impure, adulterated and misbranded foods and drugs," he wrote in a memoir. "The great bulk of the people raised most of what they ate." Processed foods appalled him; he advocated a "natural" diet composed mainly of whole grains, fruits, and vegetables.

In Wiley's time, the food avant-garde was made up of reformers calling on the federal government, which did not yet have a significant role in regulating the food supply, to establish a safe, standardized American diet. In 1902, at the beginning of Theodore Roosevelt's first term, Wiley asked Congress for $5,000 to conduct experiments on commonly used chemical preservatives. With the money, he built a kitchen and a dining hall in the basement of the Bureau of Chemistry, an imposing brick building on what is now Independence Avenue. Then he recruited from the Department of Agriculture a small band of men, choice specimens aged eighteen to twenty-nine, including a sprinter from Yale and former captain of a high-school cadet regiment, who were willing to test his belief that preservatives were harmful to human health.

Three times a day, Wiley's "boys" assembled to eat food prepared for them by Perry, a civil service cook previously employed by the queen of Bavaria. The menu was designed by Wiley, who, the press noted, "has some original ideas about feeding human beings." The food was administered in precise doses, weighed out by chemists in lab coats, lending the enterprise a theatrical aura of science; in spite of occasional pleas of hunger, no more than the exact amount Wiley had calculated would nourish a fit young man was given. More significant, the food was "pure": fresh roast beef, pork, chicken, and turkey; eggs, milk, and cream from dairies personally inspected by Wiley; seasonal fruits and vegetables, or high-quality canned goods preserved by heat sterilization only.

Into this food, Wiley slipped the suspected toxins. To test the effects of borax, he contaminated the milk and butter with boric acid and borate of soda, two varieties commonly added to meat and dairy products. (Perry asked for a raise: borax was a trickier ingredient than the salt he used to season the queen's meals.) When the men learned to taste borax and started avoiding the tainted foods, Wiley resorted to giving them the borax in capsule form. In an adjacent laboratory, their "secreta" were analyzed by government chemists.

After a month or so, some of the subjects began to feel nauseous and depressed and to complain of headaches. Two retired from the squad. Wiley had to navigate a delicate matter of public opinion, describing the men's reactions to borax as unpleasant enough to demonstrate its harmfulness, without making it seem as if he had endangered them. When one of the dropouts died, several years later, of tuberculosis, his mother blamed the Poison Squad, a claim Wiley dismissed as absurd. He did, however, conclude that borax, taken in small doses over a couple of months, or in large doses over a short time, caused many of his subjects to become "ill and unfit for duty."

The experiments made Wiley famous. "It is getting so bad that people point to me on the street and say, 'There goes the man that runs Uncle Sam's cooking school,'" Wiley told *The Chicago Daily Tribune*. "It's getting unbearable. The other night, walking down the aisle of a theater on my way to my seat, people nudged one another, pointed me out, and said, 'There goes Borax.'" (That might have been wishful thinking: most people called him *Old* Borax.) As the experiments continued, his extreme eaters were likewise turned into figures of fun, captured in songs and skits: "Thus all the 'deadlies' we double-dare / to put us beneath the sod; / We're death-immunes and we're proud as proud—/ Hooray for the Pizen Squad!" The men contributed to the caricature, divulging all kinds of details to reporters—for a practical joke, one had dosed his squad-mate with quinine found in the lab—and giving themselves the slogan "Only the brave dare eat the fare." Colleagues began to accuse Wiley of practicing "yellow chemistry."

In spite of Wiley's well-publicized experiments and the efforts of numerous women's groups around the country calling for a federal law, a comprehensive pure-food bill proved elusive.

Wiley later wrote that "There seemed to be an understanding between the two Houses that when one passed a bill for the repression of food adulteration the other would see that it suffered a lingering death." Then, in 1904, Upton Sinclair, a struggling novelist with a toddler and an ailing wife, went to Chicago on assignment for the socialist paper *Appeal to Reason*. His purpose was to write about the mistreatment of immigrant workers in the stockyards and the abuses of the Beef Trust, the six firms that dominated the American meatpacking trade. Wearing old clothes and carrying a lunch pail, he spent seven weeks wandering around the plants and talking to the men and women who worked there.

Sinclair fictionalized his findings—lightly, he said—and published them serially, taking his readers on a tour through what he called the "spoiled-meat industry." His allegations were shocking: he told of putrid hams refreshed with chemicals and sausages made from meat that sat on the floor with rat droppings and poison. The processers, he wrote, used "everything about the hog except the squeal"—a culinary boast today, then taken as evidence of corporate avarice—and labeled the scraps under whatever name would sell. Lamb and mutton were actually goat, and the recipe for "potted chicken" called for tripe, pork fat, beef suet, beef hearts, and veal bits. (Speaking to *The New York Times* later, Sinclair supplied additional ingredients: "the meat of unborn calves and cows' udders.") The industry, he said, favored tubercular cows—they fattened efficiently—and when European distributors sent back sausages too moldy to sell, the packers would remake them for the home market, using borax to hide the spoilage.

Sinclair's central figuration was that just as cattle and swine were chopped up, ground down, and exploited in every conceivable way in the great factories of Packingtown so, too, was the human labor force. His most shocking contention brought the metaphor to life. In the steamy, ill-lit cooking rooms, he wrote, workers sometimes fell into the vats, where, forgotten, they would stew "till all but the bones of them had gone out to the world as Durham's Pure Leaf Lard!" A poster for the movie version of his story that appeared several years later showed a cameo of a man falling backward into a vat, wisps of vapor reaching for him like hungry ghosts.

After being turned down by numerous publishers who thought its claims too sensational, *The Jungle* was accepted by Doubleday, Page—which sent a lawyer to Chicago to assess its validity—and came out in early 1906. That winter and spring, the papers were full of Sinclair's revelations. Here was an explanation for the tinned meat, so disgusting that a general referred to it as "embalmed beef," which had sickened many soldiers, including those in Roosevelt's command, during the Spanish-American War. Defenders of the Beef Trust resorted to embarrassingly weak arguments. "In Vats, But Not In Lard" ran the headline of a *Chicago Daily Tribune* story intended to debunk Sinclair. The deck was less than reassuring: "Bodies of Father and Son Who Lost Their Lives in Tank in 1897 or 1898 Probably Were Pulled Out and Not 'Canned.'"

Americans, naturally, were repulsed by the notion that they might be at worst unwitting cannibals, and at best rat-eaters. The country was only 130 years old; the Donner Party tragedy, in which a group of Midwesterners seeking a better life in

California got trapped in the Sierra Nevada mountains and re-sorted to eating their dead, had happened a mere sixty years before. Appetite was a site of colonial anxiety: Were Americans going to be savages or gentlemen? Would the country's wilder-ness make its new citizens wild? Civilization itself seemed to be at stake. "There can be no more important public issue than the wholesomeness of the people's food," *The New York Times* said. Sales of prepared meats dropped steeply—or so said the pack-ers, whose best political leverage lay in claiming vast economic repercussions. President Roosevelt read *The Jungle* and ordered a special investigation; his agents found no proof of tinned human but issued a report saying they'd seen men climbing over heaps of meat in dirty boots and relieving themselves on the kill-ing beds. "In a word, we saw meat shoveled from filthy wooden floors, piled on tables rarely washed, pushed from room to room in rotten box carts, in all of which processes it was in the way of gathering dirt, splinters, floor filth, and the expectoration of tuberculous and other diseased workers." According to Roos-evelt, the crisis demanded "immediate, thorough-going, and radi-cal enlargement of the powers of the government."

In the two days before *The Jungle* was published, Harvey W. Wiley, flanked by assistants carrying what *The New York Times* described as "numerous multi-colored bottles, which con-tain poisonous substances of various kinds," testified before a congressional committee on behalf of the latest pure-food bill. When the congressmen asked him about naturally occurring instances of the additives he tested—the benzoic acid inherent in cranberries, for instance—he laid out a personal philosophy of food and culture. "Assuming that the food of man, as prepared by the Creator and modified by the cook, is the normal food of man, any change in the food which adds a burden to any of the organs or any change which diminishes their normal functional activity, must be hurtful."

With the momentum generated by *The Jungle*, the Pure Food and Drugs Act, also known as "Dr. Wiley's Law," passed, on the same day as the Meat Inspection Act, which required pre- and postmortem inspection of animals, as well as inspection of all meat products, with special attention given to the rendering process. Together, the laws gave broad new responsibilities to the Department of Agriculture and began to establish an American standard for edibility. Dr. Wiley's Law made it a crime to adulterate or misbrand any food or drug sold in the country. Food was considered adulterated "if it contain any added poisonous or other added deleterious ingredient which may render such article injurious to health," and misbranded if it was deceptively labeled, not in its original container, or failed to disclose certain ingredients, including cocaine, heroin, and cannabis. The Bureau of Chemistry, guided by Wiley, endorsed old-fashioned smoke, salt, vinegar, and sugar, while coming out against chemical preservatives. Food Inspection Decision 76, the first ruling from the USDA after the passage of Dr. Wiley's Law, banned borax.

Eventually, Wiley's influence diminished—he made the mistake of condemning saccharine in front of Roosevelt, whose doctor administered it to him daily—but he continued to decry preservatives. "[M]odern housewives are veritable Lucrezia

Borgias, handing out poison from the ice box, from the broiler and the skillet, and the little tins of dinner she buys when breathlessly rushing home after her exciting bridge games at the club," he said. "The average ice box is a charnel house, which not only holds death, but spreads it." His obsession with labeling, too, was unallayed. Toward the end of his career in government, he sued Coca-Cola—he was anticaffeine—because although the drink no longer contained cocaine, its name suggested otherwise.

What is normal when it comes to what people eat? When a congressman pressed the point with Wiley, saying, "Who is to define normal food; there is a great difference of opinion about that," Wiley, the first gatekeeper of the American food supply, simply said, "I will admit that." To him, normal was the food of his rural Midwestern childhood. In 1907, he published "Foods and their Adulteration," a reference book based on his Poison Squad work, in which he denounced the "sophistication of food articles" as a crime against humanity. Intended for the ambitious housewife, the book outlines chemistry experiments that can be performed at home to detect the presence of unwanted additives and preservatives. But it is also a work of taxonomy, reflecting the cultural biases of the United States in that moment. Under the heading "Animals Whose Flesh Is Edible," he acknowledges that every animal on the planet has at one time or another been food for someone, before stating that "in a civilized community, however, except in times of disaster and dire necessity, certain classes of animals only furnish the principal meat food." He limited the list of civilized proteins to cattle, sheep, and swine. Goat flesh was rarely eaten, he wrote, "and horse meat scarcely at all."

Wiley insisted that he wasn't trying to tell Americans what to put in their mouths. "It is not for me to tell my neighbor what he shall eat," he said once. "Anything under heaven that I may be pleased to do I want the privilege of doing, even if it is eating limburger cheese." But he represented an era determined to codify our way of eating. The prescriptive attitude and the drive toward conformity were general. One of Wiley's supporters in calling for a ban on chemical preservatives was a Chicago magazine with an upper-middle-class readership called *What to Eat*. In 1906, the year of the Pure Food and Drugs Act, it relaunched under the no less sweeping but more official-sounding title, *National Food*.

The Bureau of Chemistry eventually split off from the USDA and became the Food and Drug Administration. It is responsible for policing the food supply, with the exception of meat and eggs, which are under USDA jurisdiction. "We do the cheese pizzas, USDA does the pepperoni," an FDA historian told me. Wiley wanted to return food to its natural state, and the food system to its earlier intimacy. But since his time, the sophistication of food articles has accelerated in ways he could never have imagined. The aversion to the industrialized food system that coalesced with Sinclair's novel did not lead to the system's dismantling but to its fortification, and the safety net designed to guarantee food purity is now, to some, an emblem of food corruption.

The deeper into the foodie world I ate, the more aware I became of its reactionary tilt. Though the public has embraced it as a mainstream hobby, foodie-ism is a counterculture. Its shared values are a love of the special, sub rosa, small-batch, and handmade and a loathing of homogeneity, mass production, and uniformity. Among foodies, the FDA, the USDA, and the local health department are often viewed as misguided. One need look no further, foodies say, than the slop sanctioned by the government—meat treated with antimicrobials, hormones, and antibiotics; plants grown from genetically modified seeds— to see why regulations should be ignored. For instance, the USDA approved a process called "pH enhancement," whereby beef trimmings are exposed to food-grade ammonia gas to kill pathogens (primarily *E. coli* O157:H7), resulting in a product called Lean Finely Textured Beef (LFTB), which gets mixed with ground beef. Not only has USDA approved the process, but it also distributes ground beef containing LFTB—which goes by the nickname "pink slime"—through the school-lunch program.

In foodies' disdain for the rules, there is a note of snobbery: What could the feds possibly tell *them* about food? "The regulations are designed for larger-scale businesses, not for small-scale producers," Sarah Weiner, the founder of the Good Food Awards, told me. Her organization honors "tasty, authentic, responsible" traditional foods like pickles, preserves, and charcuterie. "It makes it really hard to have a food culture."

In 2011, the Food Safety Modernization Act, the most significant revision of federal pure-foods regulation in decades, was signed into law. A response to a rash of food outbreaks that killed dozens of people across the country—salmonella in peanut butter, *E. coli* in spinach, listeria in cantaloupe—it gives the government recall powers and sets standards for safe production and handling of fruits and vegetables, even for small businesses. Some worry that it will mean the end of family farms and farmers markets, or at least prove onerous to them. In an interview with *Mother Jones,* the Portland chef Naomi Pomeroy encapsulated the frustration. "The only reason that we even need to worry about food safety is because large companies and corporations have ruined our food supply," she said.

The intellectual heirs of Wiley's pure-foodists, ironically, are the very same people trying to shield their ways of eating from the purview of regulators. "The reason there's a food-rights movement is because more and more people are afraid of the food that's available in the public system," David Gumpert, who blogs at *The Complete Patient,* said. "They want to be able to access their food privately." Stranger still, the movement's most prominent political supporter is the libertarian former congressman Ron Paul, whose 2011 *Family Cookbook* opens with a recipe that calls for Double Stuf Oreos, Cool Whip, and instant chocolate pudding.

Appetites are hard to legislate, and people usually end up doing what they want to do. The year Sinclair wrote *The Jungle,* he got his first summer cold. It was the beginning of a series of ailments that led him to John Harvey Kellogg's Battle Creek Sanitarium, which promoted vegetarianism, and to the

writings of Horace Fletcher, "The Great Masticator," who prescribed chewing your food extra thoroughly. After that, he followed Elie Metchnikoff, the Nobel Prize winner based at the
Pasteur Institute. When these programs failed Sinclair, he tried
fasting. After twelve days, he broke the fast with a milk diet—
two gallons a day, warmed—recommended by the fitness guru
Bernarr Macfadden, who had altered the spelling of his first
name so that it would sound like the roar of a lion. Then Sinclair went raw, subsisting mostly on fruits and nuts. He felt
amazing: he threw away his laxatives and went bareheaded in
the rain. In his free time, the man whose affect friends had previously described as "spiritual" found himself doing chin-ups
and standing on his head.

Fruits and nuts and milk-cleanses, though, were not food
for thought. He could jump around and never got colds but
found that the diets weren't conducive to what he called "brain
work." (He referred to himself as a "brain worker.") Trying to
write a novel while eating raw, he lost twelve pounds in sixteen
days; after six weeks, he'd lost twenty. Eventually, he discovered
the work of Dr. James Salisbury, an early advocate of low-carb
eating and the inventor of the Salisbury steak. (Salisbury steak,
according to the USDA, must be at least 65 percent meat—beef,
pork, cow heart—and the rest can consist of varying amounts of
bread crumbs, flour, fungi, vegetables, liquids, and binders.)
After several years as a committed vegetarian, Sinclair heeded
Salisbury's advice, and adopted a diet of broiled beef and hot
water, relieved by periods of fasting. At first he was repulsed
by meat; he couldn't stand the thought or smell of it. But he
came around. "I am sorry to have to say that it"—the Salisbury

system—"seems to be a good one," he wrote in a book about his dietary adventures that was published in 1913. "Sorry, because the vegetarian way of life is so obviously the cleaner and more humane and more convenient. But it seems to me that I am able to do more work and harder work with my mind while eating beefsteaks than under any other *regime*; and while this continues to be the case there will be one less vegetarian in the world."

Six

HAUTE CUISINE

For six months after our border run, Quenioux had been thinking about that pot-smoked chocolate. In his mind, he had begun to build a menu around it, with a theme, medicinal herbs, that would also reveal the yet-unknown flavors of the Chinese markets and apothecaries in the San Gabriel Valley. After a long search, he found his hostess, an elegant, dark-eyed woman with a blameless putty-colored ranch house in the hills above Encino, surrounded by overbuilt mansions on small lots and defended by a large electric gate.

On the day of the first site meeting with Quenioux and the Starry Kitchen team, she opened the door in yoga pants and a black Izod sweater, dark hair pulled back in a black headband. She had designed the kitchen at her house herself, with two ovens and a long dining table extending from a center island,

and a picture window framing a stand of birds-of-paradise and a view of the San Gabriel Mountains. Now her sixteen-year-old son had taken over and was using it to make pickles and ice cream and his current fixation, coffee. He prepared himself a cup in a vacuum siphon while drip brewed for her guests.

Sitting down at the kitchen table, she put on her glasses and opened a laptop. It was time to plan the party. How many people should come? Would it be too cold, in early April, to grill outside? Her husband appeared at the door that led to the patio and pool. His shirt was untucked; he was coming from the gym in the pool house, where there was a sauna and a Viagra clock. "You guys take your meeting and have fun!" he said, rushing past us into the house.

They talked about timing and dress code. The hostess mentioned that she didn't want her name disclosed and that the faces in the photographs should be blurred. "No social media," Nguyen said, a violation of his business strategy and personal philosophy, but sensible under the circumstances. "Are the kids going to come?" Quenioux asked the hostess. She and her son looked at each other. "He wants to, but . . ." she said. "They'll stay in the kitchen with us," Quenioux said reassuringly. They agreed: no smoking. "Smoking is so cliché and gross," Quenioux said. "Let's keep it about the food," she said.

"I'm a foodie girl," she said. "It's the circles I run in. For me, that's the whole thing." She just hadn't yet figured out how to tell her husband, a straight arrow, that the culinary event they were hosting, with food by one of their favorite chefs, was already being widely discussed as the Weed Dinner.

. . .

One afternoon, I met Quenioux at a neat white clapboard house, where he lives among collections of china bric-a-brac and intoxicating European perfumes. He wore a yellow-brown-and-green-striped ski cap and a pair of red Converse. We took my car, a station wagon—his is a silver convertible, and too small—picked up Daniel, and headed east. Quenioux had been researching Chinese medicinal herbs and was getting excited. "Some are dangerous—fatal, actually—and some have a very distinct taste," he said. "We need to gather the actual product."

Quenioux has been shopping in the SGV for years. "There I find *everything* we need for the cooking we do—sea urchin, yuzu, green tea powder," he told me once. "I can get two pounds of duck legs, no problem. I defy you to find me that on the Westside. Or some fresh blood, or a live squab—even live frogs." He gets alligator at the Hong Kong Supermarket and swears by the chicken testicles from a Taiwanese-American chain called 99 Ranch, which he refers to as "white kidneys" on his menus. "If you want to buy a pound of top round at six p.m. on Thanksgiving Day, you can go to the Chinese," he says. When he needs black-fleshed Silkie Bantam chickens, he pops out to the Chinese-Vietnamese grocery store Shun Fat, branches of which have replaced Targets and Vons and Ralphs, and which, because of the meat selection—far more inclusive than Wiley's "civilized" array—is known to some as the Dead Pet Store.

"God created a huge palate, and it's there to be picked up," he said in the car. "There is a flavor I love, that so few people do: bitterness!" He described a dessert composed of a beer fruit roll-up, beer taffy, and hops crème caramel, finished with Italian white truffles and served with truffle-barley ice cream and beer nuts. Tasting individual components, the kitchen staff puckered their lips and complained; the diners, eating the whole, loved it.

"My thing is opening up new tastes," Quenioux said. Sweet coxcombs—poached in simple syrup and grenadine to give them the bounce and flavor of a red gummy bear, and served on top of vol-au-vent filled with orange *crème pâtissière*—he counts among his great discoveries. Then there was rabbit tartare. "Nobody's ever done something like that," he told me. "To the foodie person, to eat raw rabbit is new. You develop a new taste in your palate, so it's exciting for people. Rabbit is very lean but it's full of gelatin. When it's raw it smacks." He mixed it with yuzu, chilies, and olive oil, rolled it into a ball, and tossed it in white truffle powder. "It was really so fricking good." Lately, Quenioux has been focused on ingredients like okra, sea cucumbers, cactus, and raw egg white, whose slippery textures are difficult for Americans. "I want to teach people to appreciate it," he said. "There's so much about slimy that is good."

When we arrived at Wing Hop Fung, a huge Chinese apothecary in a Monterey Park shopping mall, the Trans were waiting, Thi in gray surgical scrubs, Nguyen eating some kind of doughnut from a restaurant in the mall. She knew Wing Hop Fung's selection well: she brings her parents there to shop whenever they are visiting from Texas. She handed out a list of ingredients, including aphrodisiacs, longevity tonics, diuretics, sedatives, red bird's nest, and something called dodder, to remedy male impotence.

"The smell!" Quenioux exclaimed as we walked in, passing an impressive wine and spirits department—$2,000 bottles of Latour and Château Lafite; 1953 Macallan—on the way to a wall of bins filled with astragalus, peony root, and cordyceps, a mushroom whose common name is caterpillar fungus, due to its way of invading larvae and replacing the animal tissue with its own. (In Hong Kong, Thi said, it is steamed and served with meat.) The range of items was astonishing. Most of them did not register to me as food. There were dried fish maws, yellow as dead toenails, and deer tendons, hoof on: seasoning for congee. Quenioux held up a package of Hangzhou chrysanthemum that looked like a brick of hash. "Oooh that smells good," he said. Thi pointed them to the wolfberries, shrunken red sacs. "Twenty splashes of that for sexual vitality," Thi said. "It's good with wood pigeon." Quenioux swooned over the dung-like Chinese truffles—"A hint of chicory," he said, huffing—before stopping at a bin filled with dried apricot kernels. He scooped up a handful and let them slip through his fingers. "There's a north one and a south one," Thi said. "You can't use that much of the north one because it becomes poisonous." The menu, they decided, would have to come with a disclaimer. No pregnant women, Thi said. I looked away.

The back wall of the store was devoted to dried seahorses. Sold in $500 kits for making soup, they looked like they belonged at a crafting fair. Behind a counter, framed, was an $8,000 piece of ginseng from the Blue Ridge Mountains. Under the counter were trays of Catskills ginseng, for $1,899 an ounce.

Appalachian ginseng-hunters? The mind reeled. "The older it gets the more expensive it is," Thi said. Barrels of cheap, young stuff ($280 a pound, from Wisconsin) were scattered about the floor.

"Can we do, like, ginseng gelée with an aspic, in a consommé? Or start a soup with it?" Quenioux said.

On the way home, Quenioux continued to imagine the dishes he might make. "We have to think about ginseng, longan berries, the celery-scented thing, that risotto-like grain, the bird's nest," he said. "If I smell something, I can mix the flavors in my head."

The culinary avant-garde and the marijuana underworld have lately become intimates. Increasingly, their equipment is interchangeable. Over the years, the Chicago chef Grant Achatz has experimented extensively with scent. Achatz, whose restaurant Alinea has three Michelin stars, is trained in molecular gastronomy, the steaming-beaker approach to cooking used by Ferran Adrià at El Bulli in Catalonia, where Achatz worked briefly. Borrowing chemical stabilizers, thickeners, and gels from industrial food manufacturing, molecular gastronomy— also known as Modernist cooking—seeks to subvert the diner's expectations delightfully, using all five senses. Achatz is the most romantic of the molecular gastronomists. A Pre-Raphaelite among Dadaists, he once put dry ice in a vase with charred garlic, rosemary, thyme, and black pepper: cookout fog. Another time, he leaned hot stones against a live tomato stalk, to conjure the quintessential summer smell of walking in the garden in the morning and brushing up against tomato leaves. In 2005, right before he opened Alinea, one of his investors suggested he check out the Volcano, which he had seen while traveling in Amsterdam.

The Volcano is a squat metal cone-shaped heater with a filling chamber for "plant material," a digital panel displaying the precise temperature, and a large plastic balloon to capture the plant's vapor. Its traditional use involves fitting a mouthpiece to the air balloon and inhaling. The Volcano's manual recommends using it with chamomile and lemon balm. "We could see it would have the ability to pump out a lot of scent and vapor and capture it," Nick Kokonas, Achatz's business partner, told me. "It worked perfectly, from a culinary—and from a theatrical and emotional—perspective."

In the years since, Achatz has vaporized grass, oak leaves, and hay. "My favorite is to trick people into thinking they're eating something that's not edible," he says, such as, for instance, venison with leather aroma. His signature vapor is lavender, which he serves in a plastic balloon covered in Irish linen, under a bowl of yuzu pudding, ham *nage*, and gooseberry coulis. Before presenting the dish, the waiter punctures the bag of lavender air with a syringe in a four-by-four grid, so that the weight of the bowl releases the scent. At Alinea, Achatz's molecular cocktail lounge, the bartenders use it for the Rob Roy, which comes to the table in a plastic bag filled with lavender air. As the waiter cuts it open with scissors, it looks and smells like a new-age spa treatment. (I had a virgin one; the toasted-lavender smoke formed a film over the flavor of the deep red juice—the smell of a glamorous grandmother, covering up her snuck cigarette with eau de toilette.) When the Alinea cookbook came out, the Volcano was listed on the equipment page, along with agricultural syringes, a paint-stripping heat gun, and a refractometer for measuring sugar content in Brix. The four Volcanos in the Alinea kitchen are named John, Paul, George, and Ringo.

U.S. Customs prohibits the importation of anything used primarily as drug paraphernalia. A few years after Achatz's discovery, Customs launched an inquiry into the Volcano, which is made by Storz & Bickel, a German company. Adam Schoenfeld, who imported and marketed it, was at the time in his twenties and had recently graduated from The Evergreen State College in Olympia, Washington. "I flew around the world, I did this, I did that, I went to Thailand, I discovered the Volcano, I ate lots of cool food, I designed my own curriculum around travel and business," he told me. When Adam, whose father is the New York restaurateur and dumpling impresario Ed Schoenfeld (Chinatown Brasserie, Shun Lee, RedFarm), found out that Achatz had a Volcano in his kitchen, he sensed an opportunity. He sent vaporizers to technically experimental chefs like Wylie Dufresne, Dave Arnold, and the pastry-maker Johnny Iuzzini. "It was about expanding the usage," Schoenfeld said. Customs eventually relented, determining that the Volcano could be used as "a device to aid in a method used in modern cooking called 'molecular gastronomy.'"

"The Volcano is a multipurpose vaporization device," Schoenfeld told me one day. We were in his apartment, a walk-up in the flower district in Manhattan. He was pale and damp-palmed, with tortoise-shell glasses and purple-and-black Adidas sneakers. I sat by the window so that I could breathe. "The premise is that you use heat to gently extract the flavors, essential oils, and aromatic compounds," he said. "You can vaporize oils, plant materials. It is not sold for marijuana." Nevertheless, he has learned that when sending to restaurants he ought to send two if he hopes the Volcano to be used in the kitchen. "Almost inevitably, one makes it back to someone's living room," he said. Kokonas said there had never been an issue of theft at Alinea. "Using the Volcano is not a rock-and-roll-TV-chef thing," he said. "It's a Michelin-three-star-chef thing."

Representatives from Storz & Bickel have done demonstrations at the National Restaurant Association Show, in Chicago, and at the Fancy Food Show in San Francisco, where they trapped cinnamon-and-clove-scented vapor under a glass cloche and served it with tangerine slices. "It was a holiday scent," the representative told me. "Like spicy cookies." He was just getting used to the expectations of his new milieu; someone let him know he needed to wear a white coat and maybe a hat. Last year, Storz & Bickel made a presentation at Mandy Aftel's house in Berkeley. Aftel, a Berkeley perfume-maker who lives behind Chez Panisse in a bungalow permeated with the restaurant's kitchen smells, recently released a line of essential oils for chefs. To the presentation, she invited the chef Daniel Patterson and the food writer Harold McGee, and they vaporized marjoram—which had unexpected bubblegum notes—and bacon.

The laboratory equipment firm PolyScience started making

culinary equipment a decade ago because Philip Preston, the company's president, is a foodie. Working with the chef de cuisine at Charlie Trotter's, a pioneering Chicago restaurant that recently closed after twenty-five years, he developed an immersion circulator that became the industry standard for *sous-vide*, a way of cooking meat slowly at a low temperature in a water bath. Then he made the Anti-Griddle freezing plate for Achatz. Poly-Science also makes the Smoking Gun, a handheld tool with a chamber for burning aromatic woodchips and a tube with a nozzle attachment. Preston, who invented it, says that, in spite of appearances, the idea came not from a misspent youth but from seeing a keyboard cleaner at a computer store. "I'd been keen on adding cold smoke flavor," he said. "I thought, if I unscrewed this bit and screwed this bit, I could turn it into a smoker." When he got home, he pulled the screen out of a faucet and made a bowl out of a plumbing fixture, and sent the prototype to Dufresne, who cold-smoked lettuce with it. "Then everyone wanted one," Preston said. "Grant, Wylie, Jean-Georges, the Voltaggio brothers, Thomas Keller—you'd be hard-pressed to find a really high-end chef not using it." He went on, "It's one of those things that people look at and say, 'Oh, yeah, I know what else you could do with that.'"

The Smoking Gun costs $99.95 at Williams-Sonoma; Preston says together they sell ten thousand a year. To accomplish the pot-smoked chocolate course at Quenioux's dinner, Daniel and Nguyen went looking for something like it. At a head shop in the wholesale district, they found a poor-man's version, for fifteen bucks. It was disguised, no doubt to deceive Customs, as a vacuum for cleaning a computer keyboard.

. . .

As the technologies of Modernist cooking make their way into home kitchens, everyday American cooking is becoming more precise, complex, and refined. Products previously used for making paints, plastics, and cosmetics are becoming familiar ingredients, much as, two hundred years ago, cornstarch migrated from the laundry to the larder. "You'd be amazed how many people are using lecithin"—an emulsifier used in industrial food production—"at home to thicken sauces," chef Will Goldfarb says. Goldfarb, an alumnus of El Bulli, the molecular gastronomy restaurant in Catalonia, has a website, Willpowder, where he sells high-tech cooking ingredients. "Meat glue has become pretty normal," Goldfarb says. "We get a lot of questions from viewers of the Food Network."

This extends to people who are cooking pot at home. Not long ago, I talked to a couple, let's call them Josh and Amanda. She went to cooking school in New York and interned at a three-star restaurant there. He was a fan of *Weeds*. When they lost their jobs in 2008, they thought they'd try making edibles out of their house in Los Angeles. Their idea was to produce fruit-candy-flavored THC-laced strips, similar to Listerine breath strips. "I was looking for a way to infuse oils and turn them into a stabilized solid," Josh said. "I don't have a chemistry background, so we went down a cooking road. We came at it from a molecular perspective."

Josh had given Amanda the Alinea cookbook for Christmas. Flipping through recipes for soy bubbles and smoke gel, they found one for "Spice Aroma Strips." The recipe called for

Pure-Cote B790, a "film-forming" starch manufactured by Grain Processing Corporation, which makes corn-based products for the pharmaceutical, personal care, and food industries. Pure-Cote lends a sheen to the surface of snacks and cereals and prevents chocolates from scuffing; it also constitutes the skin on some softgel capsules. At the time, the home-cook market for industrial food chemicals was just emerging, and Josh found himself cajoling big companies accustomed to ton orders into sending him one-pound samples. When they got their hands on some Pure-Cote, they found the results too brittle—glassy rather than pliant. Josh read that the chef Sean Brock, in Charleston, was experimenting with Ultra-Tex 3, which, according to the chemical company that makes it, is a "high performance cold water swelling modified food starch." Pretending he was writing a cookbook, he corresponded with Brock, who led him to Ultra-Tex 8, which yields a pliant, paper-thin product. It became the secret ingredient of their "Medi-strips."

A few years later, Josh and Amanda were both employed again, and they quit the business. Only a couple of close friends ever knew that they had turned the apartment above theirs into a grow house and candy kitchen, where, in addition to the strips they produced all-natural, organic, psychoactive fruit leather with produce from the Santa Monica Farmers Market. Spherification being a fundamental move in molecular gastronomy, they briefly considered making pot caviar, but were daunted by the stabilization and packaging challenge. No one knew about the disposable cell phones, the Russian gangsters, or the middle-of-the-night runs down the alleys in their neighborhood, dumping roots and leaves in other people's waste bins. They had become an

ambitious, confident culinary team; they laughed when they read
the recipe for fruit leather in Nathan Myhrvold's *Modernist Cuisine*, a six-volume set that aims to be the OED of molecular gastronomy. "We had cranked out a lot more of it than they had,"
Josh told me. "Their approach was a bit basic." For dinner parties
now they serve deconstructed piña coladas with coconut strips,
minus the THC, and make pineapple glass from Pure-Cote. The
first time they ate at the Bazaar, a José Andrés restaurant in Los
Angeles known for its effortfully whimsical take on molecular
gastronomy (liquid mozzarella, cotton candy foie gras), it was
with the proceeds of their molecular edibles business.

Cannabis has been used around the world for millennia. Chinese herbalists prescribed it for absentmindedness, and
rich Romans ate roasted marijuana seeds for dessert. In the
mid-1950s, Alice B. Toklas included a friend's recipe for hash
fudge in her cookbook; it was slyly recommended as something fun to serve to your bridge group or at a chapter meeting
of the Daughters of the American Revolution. "In Morocco it is
thought to be good for warding off the common cold in damp
winter weather and is, indeed, more effective if taken with large
quantities of hot mint tea," the recipe read. "Euphoria and bril-
liant storms of laughter; ecstatic reveries and extensions of one's
personality on several simultaneous planes are to be compla-
cently expected." As for sourcing, *Cannabis sativa* grows wild as
a weed throughout Europe, Asia, and Africa; in the Americas,
the closely related *Cannabis indica*, "while often discouraged . . .
has been observed even in city window boxes."

In California, marijuana has an ambiguous legal status. The state condones medicinal use, while the federal government prohibits it outright. To get fresh leaves for a cannabis pesto, Quenioux went to a neighbor in Highland Park who has a little patch. For the rest of the applications, he sent his sous-chef, Daniel, to buy an ounce of high-quality custom-hybridized marijuana from a grow house with a white picket fence in suburban Pomona. It was the equivalent of going to the farm to meet the people who grow your mache, rather than buying it at Whole Foods.

After the trip to the apothecary, the team gathered again, at Starry Kitchen, to plan the menu. Thi had put together a list of possible dishes. "So let's go over this," Quenioux said. "Does the osmanthus have any medicinal properties?" he asked, looking at a description of a cake made with osmanthus and chestnut powder. Thi said it was good for digestion and headaches.

"I should ask my employees, 'cause they buy a lot of it—they all have medicinal cards—but how much *is* weed right now?" Nguyen asked. Daniel said his source would sell to him for $350 an ounce. "The higher potency lets off a better flavor," he said. "The lesser stuff tastes like dirt." The leaves, which are far less potent, would be good for salads and garnishes; the buds could be dehydrated and ground down to powders.

Quenioux proposed beef culotte with cannabis in place of rosemary, another sappy, resinous herb. "The whole idea is to really try to do a breakthrough," he said. "Bringing cannabis and all those medicinal herbs from the apothecary side into food."

"The fifth course will be ribs," he went on. Ginger, wolfberries, sesame oil. He suggested confiting it in duck fat. "Oh, but it's twenty-two dollars a pound," he sighed. He glanced over his right shoulder to a fountain where some ducks were swimming. Thi mentioned that they sometimes wandered into the restaurant. "Shit, you should have closed the door!" he said. "Maybe we can grab them at night."

To the matter of taste: an experimental distiller I spoke to who once, after hours, ran a couple of loads of marijuana through his still to satisfy his curiosity, said, "It's a cross between hop tones—that floral, slightly skunky aroma—along with deep, musky sage tones." He distilled it into brandy—the THC, which has an aggressive, tarry flavor, separated out—and tasted it: earthy base notes. "Then I put the sample away in the hope that someday the entire country comes to its senses," he said. His tests with straight infusions yielded more dramatic results. He drank some with friends from Chez Panisse and, he says, "I found myself stuck to the floor ten minutes later. My math was way off."

"Very vegetal, very green and bright, with just a little bit of bitterness," a bartender who used to make drinks at Momofuku Ssäm Bar, a buzzy restaurant in New York's East Village run by the Korean-American chef David Chang, told me. The bartender, who doesn't serve his concoctions to the public, uses a rapid-infusion technique to make a smoky marijuana-mescal, double charging a canister of mescal and marijuana with nitrous. The first charge dissolves the gas into the mescal; the second forces the mescal to permeate the bud. When the canister is opened, releasing the pressure, the enhanced alcohol seeps back out of the plant. He's got a friend who pairs marijuana with gin and chartreuse for a lighter profile. "It's being done all over the country," he told me. "It's so illegal on so many levels that no one talks about it openly."

As with insect cuisine, marijuana edibles have traditionally been designed to bury the flavor, hence all the cheap chocolate. Among the avant-garde, the emphasis is on revealing its taste. T., a trained cook who several years ago started Tastebud, a pot-confectionary business with his then girlfriend, a pastry chef, uses high-grade E. Guittard chocolate to complement the earthiness of the marijuana, along with butter that sometimes costs more than the weed. "Berries and herbs have an affinity," he told me, a principle he uses to guide the hard-candy flavors. (His assessment: cherry is delicious, sour apple's hideous.) "A pastry chef who had worked at El Bulli tasted my raspberry bars and went on and on about them, how the cannabis meshes with the butter, and the pastry's flakiness," he told me. "To get praise from someone who worked at El Bulli—a *Spaniard*—that was amazing." At the moment, T., who specializes in cara-mel "potcorn," is trying to source mushroom popcorn—the round-popping variety that is the industry standard for caramel corn—that is non-GMO. The idea is to add an organic, GMO-free label to his packaging for the food-conscious customer.

To Quenioux, marijuana has a piney scent, with hints of kumquat. "I would compare the leaves to vetiver," he said. Dan-iel detects grapefruit notes. "We wanted to showcase the flavor rather than mask it," he told me. To capture the essence of can-nabis in butter and in coconut oil, he fine-ground it in a coffee grinder and passed it through a sieve, reserving the crystals.

Then he employed the classic ratio outlined in the recipe for "Space Butter": a pound of fat to an ounce of bud. He cooked it slowly for half an hour in a bain-marie, carefully controlling the temperature, just as if he was making clarified butter for the restaurant.

"It reminds me of Almond Joy," Daniel said, opening the jar of coconut oil, which was a pale, greasy green. It was late afternoon at Starry Kitchen, a few weeks before the dinner, and it was time to test the dishes. The day before, Nguyen had announced that Jonathan Gold would be attending. The restaurant was officially closed, but the kitchen, a tight galley equipped only with a few electric burners and a high-power toaster oven, was full of volunteers. Daniel took two large spoonfuls of the oil, melted it in a pan, and added monkfish cheeks. Suddenly the kitchen smelled of a Jamaican beach: pot smoke and Bain de Soleil. Quenioux dumped a container of pesto made from sorrel, spinach, garlic, and fresh marijuana leaves into a pot of congee, turning it grass-green, and spooned it into bowls. I tried a bite—rich and nutty with a light medicinal taste—and spat it in the trash. The cooks lined up. "You guys are going to have to let us know a few hours from now if you feel really stoned," Quenioux said. "You have to eat the whole thing."

The morning of the dinner, Quenioux walked into Starry Kitchen with a plastic tub filled with carefully washed marijuana leaves separated by layers of paper towel. He had just clipped them from his friend's patch. "Where's my soup?" he said, and dumped a twelve-gallon bin into a pot on the CookTek induction oven. "I always said I would never do consommé in this kitchen, *ever*. But I got pushed." This one was made in the European way, with a *clarif* of wild boar, partridge, carrots, leeks, egg white, and onion, and, for the purposes of experimentation, ginseng (a blood-cleanser, in Chinese medicine) and *Angelica sinesis* (a woodsy, licorice-scented stalk, which is traditionally used as a uterine tonic). "These tastes are not recognized in people's brains," he said. "They haven't developed the taste for it, and so we added kaffir and galangal to get people happy."

Quenioux poured a handful of apricot kernels from the Chinese apothecary into a saucepan and covered them with consommé. They would confer a fresh, almondy flavor, but too many, Thi warned, might induce vomiting. "Date! I need date!" he said, and dropped nine red jujubes (for anemia) into the pan. The potential legal entanglements of the night ahead nagged at him. Nguyen, he said, had become nervous enough to get a medical marijuana card the day before, from "Doc 420," a pot doctor with her own bikini calendar. "I say, 'Well, Nguyen, are you concerned? Should I be concerned about something?'" Quenioux muttered, adding chunks of papaya to the soup.

A security guard with a walkie-talkie poked his head in the restaurant door, and everyone in the kitchen froze. A tall cook with glasses and a goatee, who was roasting a tray of partridge skins in cannabis butter, crouched down and peered through the pass-through. Daniel glanced up from a sheet of pastry he was basting, also with cannabis butter. Quenioux composed himself and went to talk to the guard. A moment later, he returned, giggling: someone had dumped trash in the wrong bin.

Quenioux melted more coconut oil on the stove, filling the kitchen with a rank, dizzying smell, and put a bowl of it on the counter. Out came the tapioca maltodextrin, a powder for making powder. He added it to the oil bit by bit, and slowly the substance in the bowl clumped. Passed through a fine sieve, it turned into a fluffy, flaky heap—pot snow, at room temperature. Daniel spooned it up and tasted it. "That's sexy," he pronounced. "That's fucking cool." Over the snow, he shook a little jar: the reserved crystals. "You have to treat it like a lady," he said, tossing it gently with a fork.

That evening, it was clear and windy in Encino. A film of pollen swirled in the pool, and the birds-of-paradise bobbed like oil derricks. The hostess had on a black dress and straw-soled wedge sandals. Her husband, who had clients in from China, had decided to entertain them at the country club instead. In the kitchen, an Irish bartender, red-bearded and thin, with pointy shoes, stood at the stove stirring a cauldron of garam masala, ginger, cardamom, hashish, and milk, which he was going to serve with dark rum. "I used to do this in Ireland as a kid," he said. "I'd take butter and hashish on a spoon and heat it up and dump it in yogurt." He opened a jar of vodka, which he had infused with marijuana using a PolyScience Smoking Gun and then mixed with a marijuana-vanilla tincture. He called the drink a Medicated Gibson. To me it smelled exactly like Dorm Room Couch.

Daniel checked the time on his phone. Instead of a picture of a girlfriend or a pet, the background image was a lobe of foie, searing in a pan. Soon the guests, shuttled by minivan, for security reasons, from the parking lot of a nearby Gelson's supermarket, started to arrive: foodies in their twenties; a porn editor; a prominent libertarian attorney and his wife, a Broadway producer; a Cal Tech neuroscientist in his seventies who had never tried marijuana before. "There's Jonathan Gold!" said a twenty-five-year-old Yelper sitting at my table. Alex and Alex, a young married couple—she a student of applied physics, he a tunneling engineer—stared at him over their *pêche* lambic, before he-Alex summoned the nerve to go meet him. "He's a really big fan," his wife said.

Nguyen came out from the kitchen. "Mr. J. Gold, you are not special here!" he announced to the room, proving that, in fact, he was. "You get to sit down and eat like everyone else." He went on to describe his idea of a plausible legal loophole. "Technically, you are here for a $150 gift and you can stay for dinner," he said.

"As a lawyer, is this legal?" someone asked the libertarian attorney. "No," he said, and smiled. He went on, "Free minds and free markets. The government says you can't eat the kinds of ingredients you want at a dinner like this, and we think you should be able to."

The soup came out—clear and musky, with a sweet, strong almond-extract flavor from the apricot kernels, and a suggestion of slipperiness from some nameko mushrooms. When the monkfish congee was served, the hostess took a delicate bite. "It's a little tingly," she said. "Otherwise it's *delicious*."

"I'd describe it as billowy," her tablemate said.

The atmosphere was billowy, too, the guests high on the promise of getting high—but not actually, some complained, getting all that high. The neuroscientist said he felt sleepy, like he had drunk a bottle of beer. A woman in a green beret scratched her back with a fork. But everyone perked up for dessert. Quenioux had scrapped the osmanthus cake in favor of an osmanthus panna cotta—creamy, with the light, floral sweetness of elderflower—which was served with rhubarb gelée and blood-orange sorbet. The plate was decorated with kumquats, tomatoes, an asparagus spear, a swish of frozen cream, and the pot snow. "What an extraordinary druggy joke!" an art historian with a pierced brow said. "It tastes like cannabis, but it looks like cocaine." On the way out, Quenioux handed each guest the "gift" that had inspired the meal, a glass apothecary jar containing two truffles and a gasp of marijuana smoke.

Food, in the foodie movement, is often treated like a controlled substance. With the Weed Dinner, Quenioux took the conceit a step further, but that was not even his point. All he wanted was to investigate a virgin flavor. He left the dinner with several dishes and ingredients to add to his repertoire: the congee and the osmanthus panna cotta, the marijuana powder, the apricot kernels. "These were phenomenal," he said. He recently made "dust" from the kernels, and served it on a dish of duck gizzards, hearts, and tongues. He told me he has no qualms about serving pot food in a more public forum, like at a pop-up. Quenioux is the avant-garde of the avant-garde; consistently, though, his peculiar fixations—ants, hearts, stolen flowers, hare—have become part of the culinary vocabulary. "I want to appreciate the marijuana, and the Chinese herbs, as a culinary device," he said. "In ten years, marijuana will be the new oregano."

PART III

DISCOMFORT FOOD

Seven

GUTS

I n the early 1940s, Maurice C. Dreicer, born on the Upper East Side of Manhattan, heir to a jewelry fortune, embarked on a quest to find the perfect steak. The meat, he determined, had to come from a happy, corn-fed, four-year-old steer. It should be cut to a two-pound steak—less than that he considered an hors d'oeuvre—at least three inches thick, and aged for four to six weeks. It should be cooked to 120 degrees—a temperature he called "extra blood-rare"—over charcoal, and be served, without seasoning, on oak not porcelain.

Dreicer's restaurant ritual was extreme. He prowled cities with a pair of binoculars fitted with a camera, which he used to photograph diners through restaurant windows, and he devised his own system of merit: to restaurants that served good steak he awarded a silver butter knife; those with "superlatively fine steak" got one in gold. When his food was served, he produced from his pockets or from the black doctor's case he sometimes carried with him a scale to weigh a raw steak, a ruler to measure its thickness, a magnifying glass to inspect the marbling, a thermometer to verify the temperature, and a silver butter knife; meat that did not yield to it would get sent back. Sometimes he brought a homemade device with two probes and a dial, which he claimed tested acidity. In later years, he added a pair of white gloves and a monocle. Waiters often thought he was from the health department. He committed wholly to the role; once, in San Francisco, he visited twenty-three restaurants in one night, tasting the specialties of every house.

His rules for consumption were, as you might expect, specific. Steak, he believed, was best eaten after an appetizer of shrimp cocktail (he mixed his own sauce from a quarter of a lemon, a teaspoon of French mustard powder, a dab of English mustard, a touch of hot sauce, and three turns of a pepper mill). Tomatoes were the only acceptable accompaniment. And, if possible, steak should be eaten alone. "Women talk too much. A steak eater should not be distracted, so he can receive the utmost enjoyment from the steak," he said. "The only way to enjoy a steak is to concentrate on it, and exclude everything else from your mind."

By 1949, Dreicer claimed to have already eaten steak in a thousand restaurants. By 1969, he had spent more than $600,000 on the project. A decade later, the restaurant count was ten thousand, in eighty-two countries. A manuscript, "My 27-Year Search for the Perfect Steak—Still Looking," at last materialized, but failed to find a publisher. Evidence suggests that Dreicer did not want his quest to end. By the late sixties, he and his "traveling secretary"—a young woman named Brigitte, who spoke English, French, German, and some Spanish; acted as his chauffeur, as he did not drive; and at some point became his wife—had relocated from New York to the Canary Islands. They spent months on end visiting fine hotels and eating delicacies, grading charts in hand. She kept thin by limiting the amount of liquid she consumed. He was the kind of man who lit his cigar with two matches at once to intensify the flavor. He once joked that if he ever did find the perfect steak, he'd be out of a job.

The figure of the modern gourmet was still taking shape in Dreicer's time. A 1961 *Los Angeles Times* piece on the emerging business posed the question "But who is a gourmet?" and said, "No clear portrait has yet been drawn." The reporter then cited Max Ries, of Reese Finer Foods, who told her that the "average gourmet customer" was forty to fifty-five years old, of moderate earning power, and preferred "to entertain at home with cocktail parties, little dinners or backyard barbecues. And for the most part these fancy food shoppers do their own cooking." What was noteworthy was that American gourmets did not employ cooks.

A student of restaurants, Dreicer longed to professionalize his obsession—and argued before the tax court that his deductions, far in excess of his earnings, did not constitute a lifestyle but culinary research. The twentieth century didn't know what to make of him. Newspapers identified him as a "professional gourmet" or as a "gastronomical authority" or as a "fellow of infinite zest and tireless intake." The tax court, which ruled against him, referred to his "epicurism" and called his manuscript a "sybaritic swan song." He was an amateur expert, a food-nerd savant, in a world that did not yet recognize this category of being. Today, we know exactly what to call him: America's first foodie.

Steak was the lingua franca of mid-century American dining and the common denominator Dreicer thought would allow him to compare the quality of food in different regions of the country and around the world. Beef consumption in this country hit its peak in the seventies. Since then, it has declined nearly forty pounds per capita a year. In the past five years, while still eating much more meat than any other country in the world, we have also cut back on chicken and pork. As meat has become a less important part of the American diet, the rituals around eating it have grown increasingly primitive. The white gloves have come off; contemporary foodies want an unmediated experience.

"It's not Bacchanalian, it's Caligulan!" the woman to my left exclaimed one night at Totoraku, an invitation-only, all-beef restaurant in Los Angeles, as course after course of raw beef came to the table. She was a member of a dining group that calls itself the Hedonists. On my right, another Hedonist, a Totoraku regular who had invited me along, was photographing each dish with a macrolens and macroflash. I felt obliged to gulp down as much raw beef throat as I could, and made sure that I was seen doing it.

In its first issue, in 2007, *Meatpaper*, a San Francisco journal devoted to exploring meat as a metaphor, identified a "*fleischgeist*": a "growing cultural trend of meat consciousness, a new curiosity about not just what's inside that hotdog, but how it got there, and what it means to be eating it." One of *Meatpaper's* founders told me that at their early public events people almost came to blows over access to corn dogs. "I'm still wrapping my mind around what happened," she said. "There was a certain kind of urgency and aggressiveness around consumption. It was a savage meat party—frenzied and visceral." She meant "visceral" literally: to a striking degree, the meat movement is about organs.

More than other kinds of foods, meat forces a confrontation with our animal natures. In his classic 1941 paper on disgust, the Hungarian-born psychiatrist Andras Angyal observed that, because it comes from a dead animal, one would expect meat to be universally repulsive, yet almost every culture on earth has found ways of accommodating it psychologically. In America, extracting the muscle and selling it apart from the animal has been very effective. "Beefsteak does not involve for us the meaning that it is part of a dead animal," Angyal writes. Cooking is another essential part of the transformation—raw meat evokes the animal more perfectly, and is therefore unappealing to many. But some animals, no matter how you slice or cook them, never make the leap from dead body to food. "This failure is best shown by the fact that in any given culture only the meat of a limited variety of animals is eaten, while that of many others is avoided as disgusting," he writes. The disgusting proposition of the *fleischgeist* is to remind the eater at every turn that the thing on his plate once lived, and to suggest that just about any animal is fair game.

Offal—the parts that "fall off" when you hang a piece of meat—generally occupies a dubious space in modern Anglo food culture. In *Charcuterie and French Pork Cookery*, the English food expert Jane Grigson wrote, "Before the war I remember hearing '*Ai* never eat Offal', spoken with emphasis and pride, a brave flicker of light in a crude waste of offal-gobblers, yet another pea felt through twenty mattresses. War shortages taught better sense. Nutritive values were proclaimed and prejudices fell, at least as far as kidneys, liver and hearts went."

In 1995, Fergus Henderson opened St. John, in London, an expensive restaurant for offal-gobblers, which made offcuts fashionable. Henderson, who thinks eating should involve what he calls a "hands-on grappling with bones," has become a hero to certain American chefs. In addition to marrow bones, he serves pluck: the heart, lungs, windpipe, liver, and intestines. According to Anthony Bourdain, Henderson's cookbook *The Whole Beast: Nose to Tail Eating* is "a cult masterpiece . . . a historic document that flew in the face of accepted culinary doctrine . . . [a] proud proclamation of the true glories of pork, offal, and the neglected bits of animals we love to eat." In the book, Henderson comes across as a nutty old nanny, blood-spattered glasses askew, clucking away about fat chunks and blood, and about how "soothing" and "reassuring" innards are. He applauds the "amazing ducky quality of Duck Hearts on Toast."

"Fergus's little book influenced an entire generation of cooks to think outside steaks and chops," Tom Mylan, who runs The Meat Hook, a butcher shop in Brooklyn, told me. Diners were drawn to its realness, the antithesis of foam. "What is more authentic than eating heart and marrow bones?" he said. "It made for an experience exclusively based on adventurousness. Only certain people could muster up the courage. Serving offal is one of the very few authentic experiences where people are going to respond with their full attention. Either you have their fascination or their complete disgust and revulsion."

A year into the declared *fleischgeist,* Animal opened. A small, spare restaurant decorated with a framed lamb's skull and a Muppets lunchbox, in an old Jewish district of Los Angeles, it celebrates the indelicate, messy, uncivilized side of meat. At first, until the din of meat-eating grew deafening, it had no soundproofing. There are still no tablecloths, no centerpieces, and no candles; it is a restaurant broken down, blowing it out before the demolition crew arrives. Animal's co-owners and co-chefs, Jon Shook and Vinny Dotolo, are in their thirties and used to have a show on Food Network called *Two Dudes Catering.* They cook an elevated version of what Gold calls "Boy Food": loco moco—a Hawaiian surfer meal, which they make from artisanal Anson Mills rice, a Niman Ranch beef patty, a quail egg, a slab of Spam, and (historically) a brick of foie—and poutine, covered with cheddar and an oxtail topping that has the texture of chaw. The place invites transgression—in fact, it commits it alongside you. Its landlord, next door, is Schwartz Bakery, and the lease stipulates that, for competitive reasons, the chefs cannot advertise as kosher. Schwartz has nothing to fear. Animal uses three kinds of bacon and manages to incorporate pork into just about everything, including the bar of dense dark-chocolate mousse that is its signature dessert, and which customers often order with a glass of milk. Shook's parents are Lubavitchers. Shook and Dotolo embraced whole-animal cookery with gusto. Grappling with the product in its least-processed form appealed to them on an aesthetic level; the economics of using every part spoke to their thrift. Nate Appleman, a proponent of offcuts and charcuterie, who by his mid-twenties was part owner of a restaurant in San Francisco, says that the only way he could afford to serve the same meat as Thomas Keller—the highly esteemed chef at The French Laundry, in the Napa Valley, and at Per Se, in New York, considered among the finest restaurants in the country—was to buy the entire beast and cook it all. Shook and Dotolo have served lamb tongue ravioli, lamb heart *paprikás*, deviled lamb kidneys, veal brains *à la grénobloise*. "What they do at Animal is use the cuts nobody wants," Appleman says. "They're really pushing the limits. They had a dish on the menu that was thirty duck hearts in curry. It was hard even for me to get through."

Dotolo—five feet six and broody, with glasses, a multicolored sleeve tattoo, and a three-day beard—is the primary architect of the menu, and he is uncompromising about his food fantasies. He has sometimes served fruit whole, without utensils, so that the customers will have the pleasure of feeling juice run down their chins. "I had this weird thing last night," Dotolo told me once. "I was, like, eating tofu and I was, like, thinking about how much it reminded me of, like, bone marrow and, like, brains and, like, that weird texture—like, soft, a little bit gelatinous. But the flavor of tofu is, like, so *yelchth*. I'll think about that now for, like, maybe a year before I think about something to do with it. I think it'd be fuckin' hilarious to do tofu at Animal, just because it throws people off so much." He thought for a second, and said, "Maybe you do tofu with meat."

One day, Dotolo got his hands on a whole lamb from a local purveyor. "I can't say who, 'cause it's not approved, but it's fuckin' good," he said. "It's all fed on apples and pears and lettuces." Shook butchered it in the kitchen. They prepared the liver with roasted butternut squash and sage brown butter, and the leg with green-garlic tzatziki, farro, and rutabaga greens. "Now I just have two tenderloins and a neck to use," Shook said. They served the brain to the chef de cuisine at the Beverly Hills branch of Thomas Keller's bistro Bouchon when he came in to eat one night. "I cut the skull open—whack!—with an ax," Dotolo recalled. "Most guys use a band saw."

The following afternoon, seven frozen pigs' heads arrived from Niman Ranch, and in the morning they went into a brine. They were for head cheese, which Shook and Dotolo were taking to a food festival in South Beach. In the afternoon, Shook, who is small and voluble, and wears boots with his shorts, opened the walk-in cooler and checked on the heads. One, in a pot, was already cooked; it was for the restaurant. "I was talking to my friend Tandy Wilson, at City House, in Nashville. I was, like, 'Man, your head cheese stays so fuckin' moist,'" Shook said. "We got real wasted and he said, 'Boy, the trick is to cook the head and leave it in the pot overnight.' So we tried it and it worked amazing."

In the kitchen, Dotolo stood over the cooked head—cartilaginous, magenta, baring its teeth—and rooted persistently around the cheek and neck for the prime bits. "We're partially professionally trained chefs, partially self-trained," he said, removing a delicate layer of skin, like a pink satin blanket, and tossing it into a garbage can. Then he tore a hunk of flesh from the jaw and shredded it with his fingers. "It's a pretty meticulous job," he said. "Some people don't see the worth in it. I think of it as the transformation of something you would never eat into something really tasty."

The food lovers of South Beach were, if not delighted, at least challenged. It was broadening by force. Shook said that everyone kept saying, "Head cheese? What's head cheese? Is that like blue cheese?" One woman, when Shook finally had a chance to explain, spat it out on the table and said, "Oh my fucking God, I've been kosher for thirty-two years." Shook giggled, recollecting. "Not anymore, you ain't!"

Before Animal, there was Incanto, in San Francisco, the first American restaurant devoted to Fergus Henderson's beliefs and a more puritanical expression of the whole-animal proposition. Incanto began as a traditional Italian place owned by Mark Pastore, a mild-mannered and reasonable man, who is extreme only when it comes to Dante: he has a special room at the restaurant where he displays a bust of Beatrice, and he sometimes dresses up as Dante for Halloween. In 2002, when Incanto had been open for a year, Pastore partnered with the chef Chris Cosentino. Now the walls of the main dining room are decorated with antique butchers' tools—splitting cleaver, bone saw, sausage stuffer, lard bucket—and the references to Dante tend to come in shouted form and refer to the nine circles of his Hell, to which inattentive employees may be condemned.

Cosentino is forty, hyper and exhausted, with a small, pursed mouth, a sharp nose, and spiky dark hair. He wears thick-framed rectangular glasses and a stirrup of facial hair that makes it look as if his jaw could come unhinged, like a ventriloquist's dummy's. Under stress, he gets blinky and pissed. His coffee order is a Quattro. The first time I met him, he was sitting at the counter at Pigg, his new restaurant in downtown L.A., where, alongside products from Boccalone, his cured-meats business ("Tasty Salted Pig Parts" is its motto), he serves Fermín's acorn-chomping *jamon de bellota—crudo*. Serving raw pork is cocky, a frank challenge to American sensibilities, and an inversion of Angyalian disgust: what should repel is presented as attractive. Cosentino dares you to eat it.

The official opening was a few days away and Cosentino was tweaking the dishes. "Layer a little bit more ear in there," he told a cook behind the sneeze guard, who was preparing ear slices with a side of brain aioli, which Cosentino calls "brainaise." "Make it look like a sandwich of ears."

He turned to me. "What do you think the culture of texture is in the United States?"

"Crunchy?" I suggested.

"Correct. What do you think the culture of texture is in Asia?"

"I think there's more slime," I said, picturing the chicken feet—bones half-enrobed in silky, fatty, gathered skin—that were my first encounter with it-is-what-it-is Asian presentation.

"Jiggly—soft—unctuous. *That's* why offal isn't very popular in this country. There's nothing crispy—unless we make it crispy." He described frying the ears and pairing them with pickled peppers, mint, and red onion. He said he expected to go through 150 pounds of pig ears a week.

Upset by the amount of waste in the meat industry, Cosentino started serving the parts Americans no longer wanted to eat: spleens and blood and sperm; lungs, lips, and livers. Embedded in his dishes are sermons on how properly to treat an animal: he serves pig's snout with escargot and watercress, because pigs in nature like to eat the snails and vegetation found near streams; he pairs wheatgrass pasta with cow stomach and intestine, because cows ought to eat grass. A few years ago, he said in an interview with *Meatpaper* that the one meat he finds too extreme is *balut*, the Filipino unhatched chick—a whole animal, eaten whole. "It was difficult, but I tried it," he said, rating it "pretty gnarly." But he believes that meat-eating should be hard. Bringing people face-to-face with the reality of what they are eating makes them more conscious of their choices, and sometimes they respond by ordering the vegetarian entrée. For a while, he eliminated butter and made his pastry chef use suet for pork-fat cookies and lard caramels. He imitated a pastry chef, whining, "I don't want to make suet pudding. That sounds nasty." Then, playing himself, he barked, "Shut up! Make fucking suet pudding."

He went on, "They call me a barbarian. They say I'm meat jihad. I just think we need to look at food in the U.S. with a more open mind." To avoid becoming a hypocrite, he takes his kitchen crew to slaughter an animal every year. Once he killed a heifer named Bertha so big that, even after she was divided between two cars, the weight of her popped his hubcaps off.

Not long after becoming the chef at Incanto, Cosentino instituted an annual Head to Tail dinner, two nights of extreme offal, prix fixe, that allow him to explore the outer boundaries of decency, manners, and taste. The second year, Fergus Henderson showed up. "That was fucking daunting," Cosentino says. "This is the first time I've cooked for Fergus. I'd met him, I'd eaten in his restaurant, I'd staged in his restaurant, but I'd never cooked for Fergus." He served a shaved tripe salad, pig's-brain prosciutto, and lamb heart. The final savory course, before a chocolate blood pudding, was a braised pig head with grilled liver and large intestine—a dish that had to go in the oven two courses before it was time to serve it, so that it could caramelize. After Cosentino fired it, John Relihan, the young cook responsible for it, approached him and said sheepishly, "Uh, chef, I, uh, didn't put the, uh, head in the oven." The dining room was full. "Now I'm backed up on what to me is the grandfather of it all. We're shitting the bed on Fergus's table," Cosentino says. Five minutes passed, and no food emerged, so Cosentino leaned through the window into the kitchen and bellowed, "John Relihan, you will give me head! You will give me head *now*! You will give me *fucking head*!" When he turned around, the whole dining room was silently staring at him.

Benjamin Ford, a chef who serves a variety of domestic hams and a whole-pig dinner at his place, Ford's Filling Station, in Culver City, says he always tries to get a woman to read over his menu and make sure it's not too alienating. Cosentino, apparently, takes no such precautions. When Anthony Bourdain filmed *No Reservations* at a Head to Tail, the menu included raw venison heart on a brioche made with pig skin; a goose-intestine soup Cosentino called "anal-ini," because, he says, "it looked like a little goose asshole"; and a dish he named "Big Brain, Little Brain": cow's brains and testicles. For dessert, he made a doughnut filled with pork-liver-chocolate ganache and served espresso brewed with pig's blood. He heated the blood until it coagulated, then strained it out, leaving behind a metallic flavor familiar to anyone who's ever been punched in the nose. Cosentino is one to force a joke. One of the dishes he is proudest of involved asparagus (a diuretic), lamb kidney (a filter), and a bright yellow lemon vinaigrette, which he turned into a fluid gel with agar and sprinkled around the plate's edge, like drops on the rim of the bowl.

Cosentino's mission is to bring the offcuts associated with poverty cooking into the realm of fine dining. For a long time, he ignored foie gras: too luxurious. But in the years following the passage of the ban in California in 2005, foie gras—fatty, foreign, soft, *femme*—took on a different aspect. Soon to be forbidden, it became a totem of food-world machismo, the unlikely *über organ meat*. One chef had "foie gras" tattooed across his knuckles. Cosentino vowed to protest to the end, right up to the enforcement date. The ban, which prohibits the sale of any product of a force-fed bird, may incidentally eliminate magret (the fatted breast), most duck prosciutto, tongue, heart, fat, testicles, and down feathers. Cosentino saw foie gras as a whole-animal issue: the duck, paragon of exploitability, was being placed off-limits. "The duck is the pig of the air," he said. "You can use everything."

In the spring of 2012, I went to San Francisco to watch Cosentino get ready for the last Head to Tail that could include foie gras. It was two days before the event, and already the atmosphere at the restaurant was wistful and charged, like a high-school graduation party. Cosentino had on a T-shirt that said "Stop Tofu Abuse. Eat Foie Gras" and a dark blue apron with white stripes. The previous day, his pastry chef had all but cut her finger off with an immersion blender, so he had taken over making the dessert: foie gras panna cotta with shavings from a frozen maple-cured foie gras torchon. The dish required forty-eight lobes, the yield of forty-eight ducks. But now he had to worry about that night's regular dinner service.

When the host arrived, Cosentino called him over. "Hey, listen," he said. "We've got a VIP tonight. Vinny Dotolo is coming in. He's the owner of Animal. Death and destruction comes upon him."

Cosentino put on his chef's coat and went into the kitchen. Like a pagan altar before a battle, it smelled of cooking meat—a nearly extinct pleasure, now that everyone west of the Hudson cooks *sous-vide*. (It's strictly regulated in New York City.) There was a digital clock, with seconds, on the wall, in the middle of a death's-head mural that resembled the flag of a motorcycle gang. "Shut up and cook," it read. In the walk-in cooler, a pig hung from a hook and hay-brined beef tendons were splayed on a rack like wet noodles. There was a bucket of foie gras, steeping in milk; a layer of orange-yellow fat had formed on the surface. Cosentino opened a box of lamb spleens, which were being pressed. "Oh, dude! See how dense and firm they are?" he said. He poked one, grayish, greenish pink, and expressed a drool of blood. He opened another container, this one full of lambs' heads, green-flecked with marinade, and still in possession of their cold, blue eyes. "Vinny Dotolo from Animal is coming in," he said. "I'm going to make him cry."

Manfred Wrembel, the chef de cuisine, a small, handsome man with a neat beard and cropped hair, appeared at his side. "We could do sweetbreads!" he said, bouncing a little on his toes. "We could confit the potatoes in tallow." He swung a bucket of duck fat enticingly.

"I'm going to fuckin' destroy them," Cosentino said again. "I think he's with his wife, though, so I don't know." Then he remembered that he had three mahi-mahi humps. "Do two on the board and one for him. That hump is going to be fatty, fatty, fatty, fatty, fatty. It's a cool set-up." He went back into the kitchen, rubbed his eye, and tasted a chunk of duck heart from a hotel pan full of gizzards, livers, and hearts.

"Good, eh?" Manfred said. "Disgustingly good?"

Cosentino started picking out the choicest bits for Dotolo. "I'm going to do best-part-of-duck risotto for him," he said. "With duck egg instead of cheese. Pain and suffering is coming."

A few hours later, Dotolo and his wife, Sarah Hendler, were seated at a corner table at Incanto. Hendler is slim and precise, with fair skin and a skeptical aspect. Her role in the Animal universe has been to try to erase in the public consciousness and hide from her parents Dotolo and Shook's reputation as stoners, enshrined in their reality show and in an early feature story about them in which their friends were depicted sticking cocktail picks up their noses and one friend tried to catch the "awful fountain" of his own urine in his mouth. She represents civilization, and she tries valiantly to hold the line.

"I like very specific things," Hendler said. "I like pasta." Before her was a plate of sea urchin and beef tendons and a plate of lamb kidneys. "We didn't order it," she said. She looked at the kidneys. "Am I going to like it?" she asked Dotolo.

"No, but you should try it."

"We went to Per Se and the waiter was shocked that I don't eat tripe or *uni,* and I'm married to this guy!"

"My favorite dish at Per Se was the tripe," he said apologetically.

Cosentino came over with the mahi hump, and Hendler gently remarked that they might have too much food already.

"I'm going light, are you kiddin'?" Cosentino said. "This is easy." He told them about the foie dessert he was working on.

At the mention of foie gras, Dotolo grew glum. Animal, he said, sold thirty orders of maple-sausage-foie-and-biscuits every night, and went through $400,000 worth of foie a year. Later, Shook told me he found the ban absurd. Like the food-freedom contingent, he considered the government's standards far beneath his own. "I think the foie gras I'm serving here is better than the chicken they're serving in the elementary schools, and the ground beef with the pink slime."

"I'm inspired by it," Dotolo said at Incanto. His first transformative food moment was walking into Michelle Bernstein's kitchen at The Strand, in South Beach, and smelling foie gras searing in a pan. "I was like, '*Wow,*'" he said.

"I don't like foie gras," Hendler said. "I finally tried the loco moco." She shrugged.

Foie gras, Dotolo said, was only the beginning of the vegan predation. "We believe that what will be next is caviar, sea urchin, and then line-caught fish," he said: the low-hanging fruit, unbacked by corporate lobbyists. "They'll never fuckin' touch the beef industry."

"Bone marrow," Hendler said. "That's another thing I don't eat. It's the consistency."

Cosentino and Dotolo bemoaned the scarcity of high-quality offal in the U.S. "All innards end up in commodity—it's so stupid!" Dotolo said. "We say, 'You kill all these cows, where are the hearts?'"

"Hamburger," Cosentino said.

"Dog food," Dotolo replied.

"It's a dirty, fuckin' nasty business," Cosentino said. "The offal goes as payment to the slaughterhouses. They bulk it up." After much searching, he said, he had found a source for green tripe—intestine stained from a diet of grass and left in its natural state. "White tripe is bleached with Clorox," he said. "Doesn't it say on the bottle, 'Don't Drink?' I'd give you a bag to take home but it's still frozen."

"I'm not a tripe person," Hendler said. "I'm a nice Jewish girl from New York City."

By 5:30 on the night of the Head to Tail, there was a line out the door. The theme of the night, chalked on the specials board, was "Respecting the Right to Choose the Meat We Eat!"

"And people don't like offal," Cosentino said smugly. "They think it's gross." Harold McGee, the food writer, was one of the first to arrive. He has helped Cosentino with technical problems over the years, such as how to pasteurize blood without causing it to coagulate and lose its color. He sat at the bar with a friend, and when the *amuse-bouche* arrived—whipped calves' brains and toast—he tapped his temple and nodded. I struggled with the brains—not with the creamy, mild taste, but with the idea of them. For me, they were, as Claude Lévi-Strauss might have said, "bad to think." The reference felt too pointed, too much of a put-down of bovine intelligence—as if the highest possible use for this young brain was to feed mine.

A few seats down sat the Dapper Diner, a heavy Asian fellow with a side part, who was wearing a lavender shirt, a striped periwinkle bow tie, a maroon vest, a silk handkerchief in the pocket of a brown sport coat, and a thumb ring. He was tweeting a picture of the menu. "I just tweet," he said. "I don't write." (His bio on Twitter, which I looked up later, reads: "I eat. My 4 basic food groups are foie gras, sweetbread, truffle, & pork belly.") It was his second Head to Tail. "Last year, he did bone marrow éclair," he said, a huge smile breaking over his congenial face. "I love offal. Other places are doing it, but not as much as here. You see sweetbreads and liver showing up more and more, but here they've been playing with it longer."

The first course was homemade rigatoni—purple from Chianti, bitter from endive—served with a venison liver sauce and the first fava beans of spring. "This is me taking it back," Cosentino had explained to the waitstaff earlier. "'I ate his liver with fava beans and a nice Chianti'—because for years when we started doing this menu they called me Hannibal Lecter." The sauce was peppery and greasy, like bits left in a pan.

Out came a fishy, deep puttanesca with a kick. In place of noodles, Cosentino used strips of pig skin, and he had named the dish 'Porca Puttana!'—a nasty thing to say in Italian.

Cosentino's wife, Tatiana, a formidable blond woman who is his partner in the cured-meats business, was also dining at the bar with a friend. "Pig whore?" she said when she saw him. "That just rolls off the tongue?" He kissed her on the cheek. "Pussy pasta?" he ventured. "It's unctuous and gelatinous and we are a country of crunchy. It's an experiment in gooey, icky, sticky textures."

Tatiana said that Cosentino no longer felt so alone. Pig ears and tripe had practically become clichés. "Now everyone's doing it," she said. "Beef heart is gateway offal. It sounds scary but it tastes like a sirloin."

After we had eaten the head, feet, heart, and spleen of a lamb, puffed beef tendons, and some oysters, it was time for dessert. The waitress delivered a shallow bowl containing a molded cream-colored panna cotta, golden popcorn, and pink flakes of shaved torchon, with strawberries on the side. The little animal-rearing lesson—and sick joke—was that the panna cotta was covered with popcorn (duck food) popped in foie fat and covered with foie-enriched caramel: extreme *gavage*, cannibal-style.

"I missed most of that, what did she say?" Tatiana's friend asked after the waitress had finished describing the dish.

"She said, 'Foie, foie, foie, maple, foie,'" Tatiana said.

One day, sitting at a Guatemalan bakery in a nondescript, mid-central-nowhere part of Los Angeles, wearing a T-shirt showing an octopus next to a bottle of soy sauce, Jonathan Gold said, "When I was an editor at the *LA Weekly*, in the mid-eighties, there was a woman who worked there and was in a lesbian meat collective. She first approached me because she thought I might have a line on where to get some lungs—which I didn't, because they're not allowed. There's too much surface area for the USDA to inspect and they're too prone to infection. But I always loved the idea of twenty women getting excited because Tuesday was going to be spleen day." Gold's colleague was ahead of her time; twenty-five years later, he said, women had finally started getting into meat. "There's a whole sanguinary thing going on that's beautiful," he said. "If women can take charge of their own sexuality, why not take charge of their own carnivorousness?"

It seemed to me that Abby Abanes, the founder of a thousand-member Meetup dining group called Pleasure Palate, had done it. Abanes is in her mid-forties, shy, with frizzy dark hair and a face dotted with small moles. She was born in the Philippines and moved to L.A. when she was five; she lives with her mother in the San Gabriel Valley. Several years ago, she decided she needed more friends and a hobby; partly inspired by Gold, she became a foodie. The first time I met her, on a bus down to Tijuana for forty-eight hours of binge eating, she was wearing an oversize T-shirt with a butcher's diagram of a pig on it. Hers was an utterly normal life, perverted by food. Since I, too, was on the bus and took part in the binge, I suppose that the same thing was happening to my life. All I lacked was the food-themed clothes.

As the first to cover the Kogi truck and a participant in the first "tasting" at Umami Burger, when it was just a BYOB one-off on lower La Brea Avenue, Abanes has achieved a modest foodie celebrity. She maintains eighty-three Pinterest boards, including Anchovies/Sardines, Bacon Love!, Avocado, Banana and/or Peanut Butter, Durian, Oxtail, Snickerdoodles, Cute Food, and Spam. When her group gathers, three or four nights a week, everybody knows the rules. "Don't eat yet!" one of them told me. "We're all like vampires over the corpse while Abby takes pictures."

One cold, clear winter morning, I went with Abanes on a Pleasure Palate outing to the San Gabriel Valley: a bunch of ladies, down to eat weird stuff. The last to arrive was Cecilia Fabulich. She pulled up in a metallic beige Prius with the license plate "DINE LA." A competitive cook, who once won the Judges' Trophy at the Grilled Cheese Invitational, Fabulich told me that Pleasure Palate members pride themselves on discovering restaurants. "We like to dig out new places. It gets really—" She thrust her elbows back fiercely. "Sometimes I write on *Chowhound,* and I have felt that Jonathan Gold kind of stalks us on there."

As we stood in the parking lot, someone passed around a small foam tray of preserved eggs from 99 Ranch. Bisected, they were like sulfurous planets, with rings of amber-colored jelly and rotten green paste, and a sludgy gray-green center. I speared one with a toothpick and put it close to my face. It reeked of a urinal. I moved it toward my mouth, but some force field repelled it, and I could not get it in. This was supposed to be the warm-up; I was glued to the bench. I secreted the egg in a napkin and put it in my pocket.

We introduced ourselves by naming the most outlandish food we'd ever eaten: *balut*; Korean fermented bean soup; *nattō* ("fermented soybeans—the more you stir it the slimier it gets"); "*balut*, blood soup, or the little worms I had in Mexico"; "the goose intestine I ate Wednesday night"; "I think I've had cat meat once." After learning that one of the women was a nurse, I decided to stick close to her. At different restaurants around the mall, we ate jellyfish, stinky tofu, and insect snacks. At a place that served steamed pig intestine and pig's-blood soup, I leaned across the table and murmured in the nurse's direction. "Are there issues about food safety?"

"If it's an infected pig, sure," she said brightly. "I've had patients who've gotten really sick." *Infected pig*: not the words you want to hear when you sit down to lunch. I turned my attention to the crinkly, golden intestine, which looked suddenly friendly.

Leaving the mall, we walked a few blocks to Nature Pagoda, a health-food restaurant with a B rating, run by the owner of a Chinese apothecary. The waitress brought two cracked white tureens to the table. One held soft-shell turtle in a broth as dark and dank as tank water. The meat was tough, like turkey, but the soup was delicately flavored with ginseng and astragalus; goji berries and gobo root bobbed on the surface. In the second was ox penis. "For the first time, I'm scared," a woman named Emilie said. She had been to medical school and had worked in the urology department at UCLA. From an herbaceous, pond-like bullion thick with sticks and ruffles of black fungus, she spooned a piece of penis. "That's the corpus cavernosum," she said—the collagenous structure that fills with blood to create an erection. At the end was a hole, the urethra. Emilie explored it with her chopstick. "That's a big hmmmmm," she said.

"It tastes like tendon," Fabulich said. "It needs Tabasco." Gold, writing to me once about some boiled ox penis *he* had eaten, had used just one apt word: *chewy.* I overcame the urge to spit it out.

Our final destination was a cute Hong Kong–style dessert shop called Tasty. Girls with long ponytails, wearing knee-high socks and fur-trimmed coats, sat in booths decorated with big pink paper camellias. After a few minutes, a waitress wearing a yellow apron appliquéd with daisies brought a glass parfait dish to the table. It contained layers of black rice, coconut milk, mango, and a translucent pulpy substance with the fragrant flavor of lychee. That was *hasma,* frog fallopian tubes. At the end of the day, Abanes said, "I'm more of an oxtail kinda girl."

Eight

OFF MENU

Conscientious foodie-ism works only if you know what you are eating. A few years ago, Dave Arnold, the genial, mop-haired food pioneer who at the time ran the Culinary Technology Department at the International Culinary Center, published a piece in *Popular Science* called "Why I Eat Lion and Other Exotic Meats." "As the food revolution continues to gain traction, our ancestral lust for robust, unusual meats is starting to spark and reawaken," he wrote, and provided recipes for *sous-vide* yak, bear, and lion steak ("57°C for 24 hours. Tastes like pork but richer"). Later, he was horrified to discover that his source—the owner of Czimer's, outside Chicago, which supplies much of the beaver, bear, and lion served in America— had pleaded guilty several years before to illegally selling numerous endangered tigers, including two Bengals, and an endangered black spotted leopard from the Funky Monkey Animal Park, in

Crete, Illinois. The meat, unloaded from a van into a back building, sometimes late at night, was, needless to say, not inspected by the USDA; according to the plea agreement, one of the animals, a liger—a lion-tiger cross—was shot and killed in a trailer in the parking lot. Czimer's sold much of this illegal meat as "lion."

The conflict between foodies' embrace of novelty and the conservative impulses of animal-rights and environmental groups is growing starker. If you are a Gold, though, the struggle is just another form of sibling rivalry. When Jonathan Gold got back from Korea, in the fall of 2008, he published a piece about eating whale in Ulsan, a port city in the south. "I am surprised to discover that the whale is delicious, leaner than beef, with a rich, mineral taste and a haunting, almost waxy aftertaste that I can't quite place," he wrote. "I am already anticipating the nasty glare I will inevitably get from my marine-scientist brother, Mark, who as the leader of Heal the Bay has dedicated his life to pretty much the opposite of this. I swear: I'll never eat whale again."

Mark responded, on the *LA Weekly*'s Letters page: "Bro— now you've crossed the line. For far too long, you have been chowing down on every marine critter I've spent my life protecting, from shark's fin soup to live prawns to bluefin to wild-caught sturgeon (largely freshwater). What did I do to you in our childhood to justify this ichthyocide?

"Now you're on to whale meat. This time you've crossed the line. IT IS ON!"

In the summer of 2009, I went fishing in Iceland and— local custom—bit the dorsal fin off the first salmon I caught and swallowed it. I got through it, with the help of a cook who cut the fin three-quarters of the way across for me, and a slug of vodka. A few days later, in Reykjavík, some of my fishing friends took me to a sleek Icelandic-Japanese restaurant. They ordered whale and invited me to try it. The truth is that it didn't occur to me to say no; yes had generally been my reflexive answer to a food challenge. The whale—I didn't know enough to ask what kind—came to the table. It was unappetizingly red, with an oily flavor that recalled the smell of a burnt wick in a hurricane lamp. My friends spent the rest of the meal talking about the high mercury content of the meat and the polarizing politics of the hunt. It all tasted like brain damage to me.

Several months later, The Hump, a Santa Monica sushi bar with a reputation for catering to thrill-seekers, was accused of serving an endangered species of whale to undercover vegan activists. The sting operation was orchestrated by Charles Hambleton, one of the producers of *The Cove,* a documentary about the dolphin hunt in the former whaling town of Taiji, Japan. Hambleton is a soft-spoken man in his late forties, with a distracted, trembly affect he ascribes to all the tuna he ate on location: he and the film's director, Louis Psihoyos, both got severe mercury poisoning.

Hambleton, whose father worked for Pan Am, grew up all over the world. As a child in Moscow at the height of the Cold War, he was forced to eat caviar sandwiches because peanut butter cost too much. Living in Antigua as a dive instructor and a treasure hunter, he ate whale with the old fishermen, and has no regrets about it. (His ethical line is that he won't eat factory-farmed meat.) When I met him recently, at a coffee shop in Los

Angeles, he was wearing a skull ring, a memento from his work as a pirate-trainer on all four Pirates of the Caribbean movies. On *The Cove*, he planned the covert missions, setting up blinds for filming the dolphin hunt, and dummy blinds to trip up the local police. When I asked him what had prepared him for the job, he said, "I was good at creative problem-solving, long hours, nasty conditions." I pressed him, and he rattled off his lawyer's phone number from memory.

In a couple of days, Hambleton said, he'd be leaving for western China with Psihoyos and the six-person Pirates of the Caribbean prosthetics crew, who had designed him a new face, with a broadened nose, darkened skin, and brown contact lenses, as well as a head of straight dark hair. Disguised as a Chinese-American buyer, he was going to film at an exotic-meat market in Wuhan, where tigers and dolphin heads are said to be sold openly, and use the footage for a television show about environmental crime-solving. Psihoyos would probably have to sit in a wheelchair to conceal his height. The prosthetics took six hours to apply and had to be worn overnight. Hambleton showed me a picture: shades of Mickey Rooney.

He told me he had heard about The Hump's secret menu from a source at Sea Shepherd, a renegade anti-whaling organization. The notion that Santa Monica, one of the most environmentally progressive communities in America, might be the site of such a blatant violation of national and international protections was alarming. Here was an opportunity, he thought, to carry on the mission of *The Cove*, with potentially more sensational results. Hambleton recruited Crystal Galbraith, a slender twenty-six-year-old *Cove* groupie with bleached blond hair and a mole under her right eye, who, he hoped, could lure the chefs into his trap.

Galbraith had read *Skinny Bitch* in college. "I was a normal eater at lunch and by dinner I was vegan," she told me. One night in the fall of 2009, she put on her best dress, a knee-grazing, tight-fitting black number by The Row, and set out to save the animals. At an apartment in Santa Monica, Hambleton removed a snap from her Guess purse and sewed a spy camera in its place. Galbraith brought along a Chinese friend who was fluent in Japanese. They settled on a backstory: they'd just taken jobs in Japan and wanted to acquaint themselves with the culture by eating the most exotic food possible. "I thought, 'This will be scary and I don't know how I'll feel, but there's no other option but to leave with a sample of whale meat,'" Galbraith told me. Her friend, Galbraith said, wasn't vegan, nor was she an animal activist. She was in it for the free sushi.

Not all that long ago, the U.S. government tried to convince people that whales, whose oil was used to light lamps, lubricate transmissions, and make margarine, were edible. In 1918, at a gathering at the American Museum of Natural History in New York described by *The New York Times* as "a conservation luncheon," the chef from Delmonico's served humpback pot-au-feu and whale planked à la Vancouver. The diners, "men prominent in scientific, business, and professional spheres," praised it: so like venison! Given its cheapness, they "were almost unanimously in favor of having whale meat substituted for beefsteak and urged its immediate adoption as a feature of the national war diet." Again, in 1943, the *Times* reported, "Whales, those greatest of mammals whose pastures comprise seven seas, will be hunted for their flesh, which will be used to help fill the gap in the nation's meat supply." The Department of the Interior gave reassurances that the meat was "wholesome when properly handled and it does not have the fishy taste which makes seal meat almost unpalatable."

Over the next several decades, the popular conception of whales began to shift, from floating oil factories to noble, cerebral beings. In 1970, Roger Payne, a marine biologist, published *Songs of the Humpback Whale*, a recording of humpback music he and his wife made from a sailboat: groaning whales, creaking rigging. Whales, it seemed, were more than beasts; they had culture. Other researchers, inspired by the findings, reported other varieties of advanced social behavior: humpbacks making bubble nets to trap their prey; sperm whales nursing for as long as thirteen years; and male killer whales living with their mothers into adulthood. Much remained mysterious, particularly about the baleen whales, which are too big to study in aquariums, but it was easy to make inferences from their large brains, complex neural pathways, and the behavior of their clever smaller relatives, the dolphins.

After centuries of increasingly high-tech hunting, several whale species were nearly extinct, and the American public began to view killing cetaceans for any reason as both an ecological and an ethical tragedy. Eating them, which in spite of the government's efforts never caught on here, suddenly struck people as barbaric. "We think these animals should be protected because they're really evolved," Diana Reiss, a leading cetacean researcher and the author of *The Dolphin in the Mirror: Exploring Dolphin Minds and Saving Dolphin Lives,* told me. "They share many of the things we do—social complexity, tool use, social awareness. They should have a right not to be killed." A collection of overlapping regulations was put in place to reflect this special consideration. In 1972, Congress passed the Marine Mammal Protection Act, making it illegal to kill whales, dolphins, and porpoises, regardless of population numbers, and banning their import, export, and sale; the Endangered Species Act of 1973 outlawed the hunt, harassment, or capture of vulnerable populations. Violations of these laws can lead to imprisonment and hundreds of thousands of dollars in fines. The 1973 Convention on International Trade in Endangered Species (CITES) regulates international trade of all whales and dolphins. In addition, since 1986 the International Whaling Commission has imposed a worldwide moratorium on commercial whaling.

The Hump was singularly well located, overlooking the runway at the Santa Monica Airport, a great place to watch rattling vintage planes and featherweight experimental aircraft take off and land. It served things few others could or would: blowfish, which contains a deadly toxin and can be fatal if improperly prepared; *keiji*, superfatty salmon babies which, before they are sexually mature, follow the adult fish to the rivers, where they are harvested. (One in ten thousand salmon caught is *keiji*, and the price can be as high as $150 a pound.) A sign on the door read "Warning! This sushi bar does prepare live sea food in full view, at the counter." It was routine to see a chef take out a live eel and drive a spike through its brain, and serve it seconds later. Live lobster was cut in half and presented with the tail meat draped over the carapace, and the head, still moving, beside it on a bed of ice. Eddie Lin, who writes an adventure-eating blog called *Deep End Dining* and frequented The Hump, said, "The effect of it is the animal is watching you eat it."

Brian Vidor, the restaurant's owner, is tall, with bushy white hair and the warm but slightly furtive manner of someone who has spent too much time in camp. In the seventies, he worked as a guide in the safari park at Great Adventure in New Jersey. Then Chipperfield's, a British circus-and-carnival company, hired him to go to the Sudan to capture white rhino calves, elephants, hartebeests, and topi for a zoo in Prague. They scouted for the animals from the air, in a small plane called a Piper Super Cub, and rounded them up with trucks, darting the mothers with tranquilizers so they would not stampede when the hunters took their young.

After that, Vidor took a job with a company called International Animal Exchange building a safari park—baboons, giraffes, rhinos, elephants, tigers—in Miyazaki, Japan. For the next fifteen or so years, he traveled all over Asia, building zoos. In Taipei, he drank snake blood in Snake Alley and tried his first insect: a Jerusalem cricket, fried with garlic and red pepper, served with beer. In Singapore, he had scorpions on toast. By the early nineties, he had become a flight instructor. Landing at the Santa Monica Airport, he noticed a "For Lease" sign, and decided to become a restaurateur, re-creating his favorite Asian street foods at a restaurant called Typhoon, where part of the menu was devoted to edible insects. Several years later, he opened The Hump upstairs for the customers who had graduated to a more morally complex and expensive confrontation with omnivorousness.

Whale consumption occupies a special place in the Japanese conscience. In *Tsukiji,* a book about the Tokyo fish market, Theodore Bestor, a professor of anthropology and Japanese studies at Harvard, writes that whales are the object of "ritual concern," mourned in special Buddhist services called *kuyo.* Etymologically considered fish—*kujira,* the word in Japanese, means "major fish"—whales were exempt from Buddhist prohibitions against eating meat. (Catholics, historically, saw the issue similarly, and allowed whale on Fridays.) After the war, when there were food shortages, it became an important source of protein; General MacArthur encouraged fishermen to convert their boats to whalers. Canned whale, mostly less-desirable sperm whale, became the Spam of mid-century Japan, remembered fondly by some aging Japanese, reviled by others as something they ate only in desperation.

But subsistence whaling, a limited, coastal phenomenon, has little in common with Japanese whaling today, which takes place on both the coast and the open seas, including in an area of the Southern Ocean designated a sanctuary by the International Whaling Commission in 1994. Under a research exemption from the moratorium, the Japanese take about a thousand whales a year, including sei whales, which have been listed as endangered since the seventies. To outsiders, their reasons can appear tenuous. Originally, government scientists justified the hunt by saying it was unavoidable: in order to collect the tissue necessary for DNA analysis—a tool for understanding stock structure—the whales had to be killed. Now that it is possible to biopsy living whales, they say that they need to examine their stomach contents for proper ecosystem management. The hunt, which is accomplished by firing an exploding harpoon at the whale, is considered by many to be inherently inhumane. In any case, U.S. scientists have a hard time finding anything useful in the Japanese data, because the whalers go only where they know the whales to be, and they do not carry scientific observers aboard.

Japanese pro-whaling politicians and organizations insist that whale stocks are healthy, and characterize the opposition as "culinary imperialism." The government spends copiously to support the hunt—reportedly some $45 million in 2011, including funds intended for tsunami relief—though it struggles to find a market for the meat, which, according to the terms of the research exemption, it is obligated not to waste. In 2008, the government sold ten tons of whale at a discount to schools in Yokohama for Traditional School Lunch Week. Homey, old-fashioned, and not particularly prestigious, the meat nonetheless commands a high price at specialty all-whale restaurants, where everything from tongues to testicles are served. The tastier tail and belly cuts of the rarer baleen whales are sometimes available at fancy sushi bars. But a poll conducted by the International Fund for Animal Welfare in early 2013 showed that only 10 percent of Japanese had eaten whale in the previous year.

How to explain a circular, propped-up, ecologically dubious, economically precarious industry—other than to say that's what happens when governments get too involved with the food business? Subterfuge. "The whale industry has nothing to do with whales," Casson Trenor, a former Sea Shepherd activist who in 2008 started what he believes to have been the world's first sustainable sushi bar, Tataki, in San Francisco. (Now you can eat sustainable sushi in Boise.) "It has to do with drawing a line in the sand about national sovereignty and resource management," he said. "The idea of other countries being able to determine what can and can't be taken from the ocean is anathema to the Japanese." To this way of thinking, Japan has created a baffle to distract Western conservation groups from the fishery it truly wants to shield from interference: bluefin.

When they got to the restaurant, Galbraith chose a seat facing away from the bar and placed the purse with the camera in it on the table. On the chair next to her, she put her friend's purse, which had a gallon-size ziplock bag inside it. They ordered *omakase,* chef's choice. After they had been eating for a few hours, her friend asked the waitress, in Japanese, for whale: *kujira.* According to Galbraith, it came to the table, sliced very thin, on a glass plate, with special soy sauce, accompanied by several pieces of dark reddish-brown sashimi that the waitress identified as horse, which has been illegal to serve to people in California for more than a decade. Galbraith's friend, who was seated facing the bar, had her leg pressed against Galbraith's; she moved it away whenever the chefs were watching. The women tasted both kinds of sashimi, while the chefs studied their reactions intently. As soon as the chefs turned away, Galbraith's friend touched her leg again, and Galbraith secreted two pieces of each kind of meat in a napkin, which she slipped into the ziplock. They left with a handwritten receipt, which included the words *whale* and *horse*, in English. The price for that course alone was $85.

Hambleton took the meat, froze it, and the following morning sent it by courier to Dr. Scott Baker, the associate director of the Marine Mammal Institute at Oregon State University, and an expert in cetacean molecular genetics. Baker, who recently established a database of whale, dolphin, and porpoise DNA, and has sampled cetacean meat sold in markets throughout Japan and Korea, identified the meat as sei, the fourth-largest of the baleen whales, behind blues, fins, and rights. Fast, sleek, and elusive, sei whales live far offshore and can travel at speeds up to thirty-five miles an hour. Baker called the National Oceanic and Atmospheric Association, which enforces the Marine Mammal Protection Act.

A few months later, federal investigators asked Galbraith to return to The Hump to collect more samples. Her Chinese friend had refused to go back, afraid that the *yakuza* were involved and might come after her, so Galbraith brought another friend, Heather Rally, a petite, part Asian woman in her early twenties. Hambleton tricked out the Guess purse with a better camera, from a top designer of surveillance equipment in New York, who helped with *The Cove* and, Hambleton told me, works with Israeli intelligence. "A lot of the cameras we get before the military does," he said.

Again the women ordered *omakase*, and when they asked

specifically for whale they were allegedly served a plate of it. While they ate, Psyihoyos, who was in town getting ready for the Academy Awards, sat with Hambleton in an SUV in the parking lot, monitoring the audio feed. The filmmakers were as excited as they were appalled. "You could hear the live fish flapping at the table next to them!" Psihoyos told me. "The idea of taking apart a live animal for culinary enjoyment—now we're out of the food world and into the world of snuff films."

Meanwhile, a pair of agents from NOAA and the U.S. Fish and Wildlife Service had set up a base of operations at the Beverly Hills estate of an animal-loving former rock-and-roll manager. Leaving the restaurant with more samples, Galbraith and Rally headed to Beverly Hills. The house, vast and contemporary, with a waterfall, a room with a piano and eight guitars, and an extensive art collection, was also home to six rescue dogs. The agents turned a guest bathroom into a lab and tried to ignore the fact that the owner of the house, who had a serious medical condition, was walking around with a joint. "The look on their faces was great, like, 'Keep that away from us,'" Hambleton said.

In the bathroom, the agents worked late into the night debriefing Galbraith and Rally and preparing the samples. Hambleton secretly kept a little meat for himself; he didn't trust the feds to resist political pressure if someone decided it would be inconvenient for U.S.-Japan relations to find sei whale for sale in the United States. But he didn't have cause to use it: the NOAA lab the meat was sent to identified it as sei, too.

In early March 2010, the investigators asked Galbraith and Rally to make a final trip to The Hump. This time, the agents checked their purses before they went in and planted three of their own—from NOAA, Fish and Wildlife, and U.S. Customs and Border Protection—at the sushi bar. From the parking lot, Hambleton and Psihoyos listened to Galbraith and Rally and relayed information to them and to an agent stationed in the parking lot.

"They are ordering blowfish," Psihoyos texted one of the agents at the bar. The agents replied that there was only one chef in America licensed to prepare it, and he was based in New York. Then, "They were just served horse." Several minutes later, Psihoyos wrote again. "Just served the blowfish. What could possibly go wrong?"

After mackerel, toro, sea urchin, kobe beef, and sweet shrimp, Galbraith and Rally requested *kujira* by name. According to the affidavit, as the chef left to go outside, the Fish and Wildlife agent followed him and watched from a stairwell while he appeared to walk away from an old white Mercedes in the parking lot, carrying a hunk of meat wrapped in clear plastic.

"Nice," the agent in the parking lot texted Psihoyos.

"Bingo!" he responded.

Trailing the chef back inside, the agent who had been in the stairwell said he saw the chef slap it on the sushi bar in front of an underling, who cut it into small strips. Then, the agent said, he and his colleagues instigated speculation among the other patrons at the bar as to what kind of meat it was. Finally, the chef slicing it muttered "whale," at which point it was delivered to Galbraith and Rally.

Of all the things she ate in the name of saving animals, Galbraith found the alleged horse meat most disturbing. "Everything else was so good," she said. "I feel guilty saying it." Whale had the strange but not unpleasant flavor of "fishy beef," but horse she found altogether unpalatable. "It was pungent and gamey, really disgusting." she told me. To eat it, she had to fool herself back into a pre–*Skinny Bitch* mentality. Self-deception, as it happened, was not the only trickery at work on Galbraith's visits to The Hump. So committed was the restaurant to serving the outrageous and off-limits and hard-to-source that it resorted to a little subterfuge of its own. When Scott Baker's DNA tests came back, the horse that had assaulted her palate with its strangeness was revealed to have been beef.

A few days after *The Cove* won the Academy Award for Best Documentary Feature, The Hump's chef, Kiyoshiro Yamamoto, and Typhoon Restaurant, Inc., Vidor's company, were charged with violating the Marine Mammal Protection Act. People were shocked. "Short of putting human body parts on the menu, there isn't anything worse than serving whale to restaurant customers," Mark Gold wrote on his blog, *Spouting Off*. The invocation of cannibalism got my attention. It smelled of unexamined xenophobia: only a sub-human monster would eat another person. More important, it confused the nature of the issue, which is a problem of quantity not kind. Jonathan Gold, for his part, didn't take his brother's bait. He merely linked to his piece about eating whale in Korea.

An apology posted on The Hump's website doubled as a defense of culinary relativism. "The charge against the restaurant is true," it said. "The Hump served whale meat to customers looking to eat what in Japan is widely served as a delicacy." The message also said that The Hump would close, donate to conservation organizations, and pay whatever fine the court might deem appropriate (usually $100,000 for individuals and $200,000 for businesses). But then the charges against the restaurant and Yamamoto were abruptly dropped. Vidor, when I asked him about it in 2011, said he couldn't discuss the case. Prosecutors filed a separate charge—a misdemeanor—against the supplier, from whom, they claimed, Yamamoto had been getting whale for years. Using genetic information, Baker was able to trace the whale served at The Hump definitively to the Japanese scientific hunt.

At the end of 2012, a friend of mine told me that Yamamoto had opened Yamakase, a secret sushi bar with an unlisted phone number and address, accessible, according to its website, by invitation only. My friend had often entertained Japanese clients at The Hump. He told me stories of staying late, after all the other customers left, when the chefs locked the door and pulled out the strange stuff—tiny bright green turtles, rattlesnake moonshine—from coolers underneath the bar. He knew Yamamoto well enough to get us in. He also knew to bring enough sake to share with him. When we arrived, Yamamoto was standing outside, smoking a cigarette on an otherwise empty street. The restaurant, a onetime gelateria next to a place advertising itself as "Home of the Pregnant Burrito" had papered-over windows; behind them, a row of traditional narrow-necked bottles showed in silhouette, like a Morandi. The sign on the door said "Closed." It was the seafood equivalent of Totoraku, the invitation-only beef restaurant where I'd gone with the Hedonists, and in fact

Yamamoto and the beef chef, Kaz Oyama, are great friends: the white Mercedes from which Yamamoto allegedly took the whale was registered to Oyama.

Inside: nine seats before a sushi bar, a glowing pink lump of Himalayan salt, and a gigantic, bristling Hokkaido crab with the face of an Irish brawler. Yamamoto had opened specially for us, and we were the only customers. He went behind the bar and sliced a piece of Japanese *wagyu* into sheets, grated a little salt on them, and seared them lightly. The ban on importing Japanese *wagyu* had just been lifted. "Only two weeks it's been available," he said when he looked up. "It's not on the open market yet." He offered to get us some to have at home.

We ate the beef, we ate the crab, we ate gumball-size baby peaches, olive-green and tasting like a 1940s perfume. There was slippery jellyfish in sesame-oil vinaigrette, and a raw oyster, poached quail egg, and crab guts, meant to be slurped together in one viscous spoonful. That dish—quiver on quiver on quiver— epitomized the convergence of the disgusting and the sublime typical of so much foodie food. It was almost impossible to swallow it, thinking ruined it, and submission to its alien texture rewarded you with a bracing, briny, primal rush.

"*Damn* good!" Yamamoto, a solid, gruff guy with bushy eyebrows, said, and took another swig of sake.

The restaurant was authentic and obscure, and demanded special willingness and stamina on the part of the eater. One influential blogger, who posted about eating twenty-six courses there with the French chef Ludo Lefebvre, wrote, "I think Yamakase's going to be the next big thing on the Japanese scene here in LA. I'm already thinking about my return trip—it's that good. Seriously though, if you care at all about Japanese dining, you owe it to yourself to give this place a try, *if* you can get in of course."

But in early 2013, Susumo Ueda and Yamamoto were indicted, along with Typhoon Restaurant, Inc., on charges that they conspired to smuggle and sell whale meat; Yamamoto was also charged with interfering with the investigation. This time the penalties were potentially severe: up to sixty-seven years in prison for Yamamoto and ten for Ueda, and a fine of $1.2 million for Typhoon Restaurant, Inc.

On the day of Ueda's arraignment, I went downtown to the Federal Building. In the hallway outside the courtroom, I noticed a young Japanese woman with a long black ponytail, shushing a baby. It was Ueda's wife, Yukiko; I went over to introduce myself. She said that her husband now had a job working at a sushi bar in Beverly Hills. "It's more conventional," she said. "Not so interesting as at The Hump. But you can call in advance. If he knows you're coming he will order something special for you."

Ueda, a kind-looking man with a graying buzz cut and a short goatee, used a Japanese interpreter to enter a plea of not guilty. Sei's status as an endangered animal was a legitimate source of outrage, but it wasn't the legal matter at issue; the law the chefs and the restaurant were charged with violating covers all cetaceans, endangered and not. In a sense, they were accused of not understanding that in America whales and their relatives are considered too smart—too human-like—to eat.

Brian Vidor built his businesses around the thrill of eating the forbidden: tiny insects downstairs, massive endangered species upstairs. One place represented rapacious, selfish, greedy devouring of all the world's creatures, the other broad-minded, virtuous, global humanism; one was theoretically sustainable, one likely not; both challenged notions of what is appropriate food. Vidor's lawyer entered a not-guilty plea for Typhoon Restaurant, Inc., too. After leaving the courtroom, he summed up his client's position and, as far as I could tell, the attitudes of the adventurous foodies who ate there and distanced themselves when the dark side of their thrill-seeking was exposed. "He owned the restaurant, but he's a Caucasian, he's a fun-loving guy—he wasn't involved day to day."

As a culinary prospect, horse presents a different problem to Anglo eaters. It is too familiar a creature for them to eat comfortably. But eat it they do. In early 2013, Tesco, the British supermarket chain, made a startling revelation: some of its frozen beef patties contained horse meat, one sample as much as 29 percent. Then Burger King, which used the same Irish supplier (who put the blame on *its* supplier, in Poland), admitted that its meat was potentially contaminated, too. A British food manufacturer disclosed that its beef lasagna was purely horse. Ikea pulled its meatballs—horse—from locations across Europe. For Americans who worried that something similar might happen here, it was hard to say what was more disconcerting, the idea that you wouldn't be able to taste the horse, or that you would. Foodies had the opposite reaction. Canada's CBC News reported that they were rushing to try it.

Horse meat is red, bloody, unmarbled, and is said to be

reminiscent of venison (venison, apparently, is the chicken of the alt-meat world). It takes a lot of grass to make a little bit of horse; given a choice, people have preferred to use horses as work animals, for transportation, and as instruments of war. In the first millennium, the Catholic Church, threatened by the stubborn pagan habit of ritual horse-eating—it was tied to Odin worship in Germany and Northern Europe—took the unusual step of banning it. Mostly, the ban was successful; only Iceland, which made exemption from the ban a condition of conversion, persisted.

Smart people have been making a logical argument in favor of horse meat for centuries. Parisians discovered it the hard way, as a food of last resort during the Revolution, but by the mid-nineteenth century—just in time for the Siege of Paris, when it came in handy again—intellectuals were promoting it as a cheap, nutritious, and tasty solution to the problem of hunger. The French zoologist Isidore Geoffroy Saint-Hilaire, who championed the cause, recommended horse by saying that "it has been sold in restaurants, even in the best, as venison, and without the customers ever suspecting the fraud or complaining of it." In *The Curiosities of Food*, published in 1859, Peter Lund Simmonds, a British journalist who fashioned himself as a Victorian-era Herodotus, reported, "Horse-flesh pie, too, eaten cold, is a dainty now at Berlin and Toulouse, and boiled horse, *rechauffé*, has usurped the place of ragouts and secondary dishes!" But trusty, tin-eared Anglo-Saxon—"horse-flesh pie"—was not the way to introduce the delicacy that, Simmonds said, was "at the present the rage" in Europe's dining clubs and salons. At home in England, members of the Society for the Propagation of Horse Flesh as an Article of Food hired French chefs to prepare banquets of *chevaline*. Previously, the English had known *chevaline* by the name "cat food."

Anxieties about sustainability also prompted another intellectual, Calvin W. Schwabe, the "father of veterinary epidemiology," to urge a reconsideration of the obvious, spurned protein. In 1979, he published *Unmentionable Cuisine,* which he described as "a practical guide to help us and our children prepare for the not too distant day when the world's growing food-population problem presses closer upon us and our overly restrictive eating habits become less tolerable." The taste for horse, he wrote, was "superficially latent" in many Americans. Case in point: a horse-meat shop in Westbrook, Connecticut, that opened during a period of high beef prices in the early seventies and was hugely successful. "I'll sell it as long as it moves," the proprietor told a reporter amid brisk sales on opening day, a cavalry of mounted protestors outside his door. Schwabe provided a recipe for meat loaf—three parts horse to one part pork—he and his wife made often during his years in vet school.

Horse advocacy groups have long pressed for a federal ban on horse slaughter, arguing that horses are companion animals and therefore should not end their lives as food. The "Americans don't eat pets" argument strikes me as a weak one, rooted in denial. Who's to say what is a pet, or under what circumstances? Besides, it's a standard that is unevenly applied. The rose-haired tarantula Daniella Martin made into sushi came from a pet store and was likely intended to be a friend for an introverted twelve-year-old, but inspired no extra sympathy as a result.

At the turn of the twenty-first century there were only three horse slaughterhouses operating in the United States, all foreign-owned, with all the meat going to Europe and Japan. In 2007, the last of them closed, and USDA inspections were struck from the federal budget, effectively banning domestic slaughter. Over the next five years, hundreds of thousands of live horses left America to be slaughtered in Canada and Mexico, under conditions advocates of domestic slaughter and animal-rights groups alike deplored. A report by ProPublica suggested that, in spite of laws against the practice, some of them might have been wild horses captured by the Bureau of Land Management in roundups and sold to "kill buyers"; others came from racetracks and were full of steroids, anti-inflammatories, and other medications prohibited in food animals.

In 2012, funding for USDA inspection was restored, and various companies have announced plans to open slaughterhouses. While the majority of the market will likely be foreign, boosters are making a direct appeal to adventurous American foodies, on the basis of the other exotic foods they have accepted. "The Promise of Cheval," a document recently produced by the International Equine Business Association, asks, "In a country where common gastronomic choices include everything from baby lambs and suckling pigs to grasshopper tacos and alligator tails, why can you not find the horse steak that was available on the menu of the Harvard dining room in the 1990s?" (The Faculty Club served it, with mushroom sauce and vegetables.) It goes on to describe a cheap, sweet, red meat, just out of reach. "When our Canadian neighbors are dining on delightful meals of Cheval au Porto, where is the same lean, tender dish to tempt our palates?" When I talked to Sue Wallis, a state legislator in

Wyoming who is trying to open a slaughterhouse in Missouri, she said, "There's great action going on with artisanal meats and butchery, and I think *cheval* would be interesting to those folks." Wallis is also a raw-milk advocate. Her favorite, of course, is raw horse milk, which she has tried courtesy of an Amish farmer who sells it to the cosmetics industry but holds some back to drink with his family.

The history of accidental horse-eating is long. Simmonds, in *The Curiosities of Food,* remarked that no one in the English knackers' yards could account for the hearts and tongues, and suggested that the "ox-tongues" sold as Russian imports might be equine instead. Upton Sinclair put it on par with the other horrors depicted in *The Jungle,* revealing that, until public outrage temporarily put a stop to it, the packers, in addition to all their other crimes against purse and palate, were slaughtering and tinning horses. At the turn of the last century, *The New York Times* reported frequently on a German butcher named Henry Bosse, "of horse-bologna-sausage fame," who operated a slaughterhouse beside the racetrack in Maspeth, Long Island. His business was "transforming decrepit quadrupeds into odiferous bologna sausages" for shipment to Belgium and Germany. Sometimes, the paper alleged, "after the horse meat was shipped to Europe and manufactured into sausage it was resent to this country and sold as some of the famous brands."

Hugue Dufour came by his "horse-bologna-sausage fame" differently—by openly appealing to the outré tastes of foodies. Dufour, who is Canadian, grew up on a working farm; sometimes the family slaughtered and ate their horses. Before coming to New York, he worked for Martin Picard at Au Pied du Cochon, in Montreal. The restaurant is known for its hedonistic foie gras and whole-animal frenzies: Animal plus Incanto. In an idiosyncratic homemade cookbook, *Au Pied de Cochon Sugar Shack*, Picard chronicles a sugaring season at a maple orchard forty-five minutes outside of town, where he has a second restaurant. Among photographs of syrup-immersed bacchantes and detailed instructions on how to make squirrel sushi, he writes, "I LOVE carcasses! I like tearing them apart and picking them clean with my fingers and I don't feel the slightest bit shy about doing it in public."

Au Pied du Cochon avoided serving beef, which it saw as the product of a wasteful, unwholesome industry. Under Picard, Dufour learned to cook red deer, venison, bison. Although the restaurant did not serve horse, he began to wonder about it. The stuff he'd eaten as a kid had not been good; he wanted to see if as a chef he could make it delicious. "It has long ribs so you can do a very Flintstoneish rack that's kind of cool," he said. He played around with tartare, a classic presentation—and the Tatars ate their horses, too. Ultimately, he decided that the leanness of the meat made it ideal for charcuterie.

In the spring of 2012, Dufour, by this time living in New York, was invited to participate in the Great Googa-Mooga, a food festival in Prospect Park, and was given a booth in Tony's Corner, an area overseen by Anthony Bourdain. "It's supposed to be the big foodie happening, so let's see how far foodies can go," Dufour recalled thinking. He sourced some horse from a friend with a slaughterhouse in Canada, and imported it legally, with the knowledge of the health department. His offering was a grilled horse-bologna, cheddar, and foie gras sandwich. At his booth, there was a horse cutout—you could stick your head through and get a picture taken. How's that for identification with your meal?

It was a moment of truth for the self-selected contingent that ventured over to Tony's Corner. "The foodies got torn," Dufour said. "Should I go for horse meat or should I not be a foodie?" Five thousand of them went for it. When the VIP section ran out of food, the organizers came to him to beg for horse.

For Dufour, the bologna was exploratory; he wanted to see what the public could tolerate. He was happily surprised. "They loved us so much," he said. "I was, like, 'New Yorkers are great. They have no problem with horse meat. Let's do it.'" Soon afterward, he announced that he would serve horse tartare at M. Wells Dinette, the new restaurant he was opening at MoMA PS1 in Queens. The response was so virulent—angry callers told him he didn't deserve to live in America and should leave—that he wrote a statement saying that he would drop the tartare from the menu. His motive, he wrote, had merely been to "offer customers new things," beyond the trinity of beef-chicken-pork. He went on, "It was certainly not our intent to insult American culture. However, it must be said, part of living in a city like New York means learning to tolerate different customs." Then he invited his critics to come in for a drink "and a bite of whatever animal they do consume (if any)"—which included, at the time, foie gras bread pudding, escargot and bone marrow, and blood pudding.

"Maybe the whole foodie counterculture is a reaction to the

oppression of just a few things to eat and big supermarkets where you find everywhere the same thing," Dufour said. "For me, eating other animals, including horses, is a responsible thing to do. If you like meat, it's trying to find other sources, meat that is already around that would otherwise go to waste." Because it's not raised for human consumption, the meat sometimes poses a health risk—but, he says, so do conventionally raised beef and poultry. He finds the sentimental argument weak and insupportable. "It's more like recycling a dead animal," he said. "We can't start burying horses with tombstones every time."

For his next restaurant, M. Wells Steakhouse, Dufour envisions a "meat temple," where he will serve a zoo's worth of birds and beasts, and forgotten cuts of familiar animals. "When I call my butcher I ask for whatever people don't want, what's cheap, and make it nice," he said. His plans call for a wood-fired grill, next to a concrete trough filled with lobsters, trout, sea urchins. "Everything crawling and live," he said. "I grab and butcher them real quick and grill them really quickly." From time to time, he hopes to have exotic meats like rattlesnake and lion, which he imagines serving in a black peppercorn sauce. "I would have loved to do horse," he said ruefully.

Most people hold back some species or another from consideration as food, and the reasons can seem arbitrary. Usually it seems to come down to relatability. But to be upset only about the animals we identify with leads us, helpless, toward hypocrisy. Diana Reiss, the dolphin researcher, isn't vegetarian, and she has her doubts. "Different cultures have different accepted animals to eat," she says. "How do we grapple with that?" One former Hump regular I spoke with said he refuses to eat anything too smart, but, when it comes to pigs, he just avoids thinking about it, because he loves eating them so much. "In a perfect world, I'd be a vegetarian," he said. When I told Vidor, a snake-blood-drinker and scorpion-eater who closed one of his restaurants after admitting to serving an endangered mammal, that I had eaten dog in Vietnam, he was aghast. "See, I wouldn't eat dog," he said, withdrawing self-protectively, as if I might bite his hand.

For myself, I began to feel that the principle I had eaten by—I'll try anything once—was inadequate to the times. Foodie-ism is pushing things too far and too fast for that. I felt a new line etching itself on my conscience. The Tailless Whip Scorpion Rule was: Don't be the first to try something. After thinking about The Hump, I arrived at a new criterion for consumption: Don't be the last.

Nine

THE HUNT

At Starry Kitchen on the night of the *escamoles*, I struck up a conversation with a young chef named Craig Thornton, who was at the table next to me. He had on a camouflage hat and black T-shirt and was eating dinner with Eva Card, a dark-haired actress who models for women's magazines and was his girlfriend at the time. Habitual extreme eating had led her to conclude that ignorance was to be preferred. "I probably wouldn't have eaten it if I'd known what it was," she said about the ant pupae. "I don't ask anymore." Thornton said he'd had *escamoles* a bunch of times, and had even served them. "It's hard to find a clean source, though, and I'm very, very particular," he said. In order to find goat that meets his standards, for example, he drives to a farm forty miles east of L.A. and kills it himself. "When you're killing something, you have a whole new outlook," he said. Scarcity was on his mind, and the developing world's demand for meat. "I get more and more paranoid about food. It's affecting the way I'm cooking. I'm cooking thinking about the future of food rather than thinking about right now," he said. He was planning to start a hydroponic garden so he'd have more control over his produce. I asked him where his restaurant was. "My apartment," he said.

Jonathan Gold's ideal restaurant is one where people cook personal, home-style food in an intimate setting with the weird music they like and their strange art on the wall. For him, this means the "traditional" restaurants of Los Angeles: unassimilated ethnic cooking intended for a narrow audience. Thornton also cooks what he likes, on his own terms, for a tiny, very specific group; it's his music on the stereo, his bedroom just beyond that makeshift door. Here, I thought, was a chance to look unobstructed at the new American cooking that is taking shape. With no health department to worry about and no investors to please, and an audience made up of adoring foodies who have sometimes waited years for a spot, the features of the movement would be laid out plain.

Several nights a week, a group of sixteen strangers gathers around Thornton's dining-room table to eat delicacies he has handpicked and prepared for them, from a meticulously considered menu over which they have no say. It is the toughest reservation in the city: when he announces a dinner, hundreds of people typically respond. The group is selected with an eye toward occupational balance—all lawyers, a party foul that was recently avoided thanks to Google, would have been too monochrome—and, when possible, democracy. Your dinner companion might be a former UFC heavyweight champion, Ludo Lefebvre, a foodie with a Lumix, or a kid who saved his money and drove four hours from Fresno to be there. At the end, you place a "donation"— whatever you think the meal was worth—in a desiccated crocodile head that sits in the middle of the table. Most people pay around $90; after buying the ingredients and paying a small crew, Thornton usually breaks even. The experiment is called Wolvesmouth, the loft Wolvesden; Thornton is the Wolf. "I grew up in a survival atmosphere," he says. "I like that aggressiveness. And I like that it's a shy animal that avoids confrontation."

Thornton is known never to prepare a dish the same way twice, an ideal conceit for the age of social media that also speaks to his nimbleness and resourcefulness, his hunter's sense of opportunity. From above, the food—smeared, brushed, and spattered with sauces in safety orange, violet, yolk yellow, acid green—is as vivid as a Kandinsky; from the table's edge, it forms eerie landscapes of hand-torn meat, loamy crumbles, and strewn blossoms. Being presented with a plate of Thornton's food often feels like stumbling upon a crime scene while running through the woods. A recipe for Wolves in the Snow, a dish of venison with cauliflower purée, hen-of-the-woods mushrooms, beetblackberry gastrique, and Douglas-fir gelée, which Thornton published in the *LA Weekly*, instructs, "Rip venison apart with two forks, which will act as sharp teeth. . . . Attack the plate with your blackberry beet 'blood.'"

He introduces his courses with minimal fanfare, rattling off the main components almost dismissively. "This is rabbit, with poblano pepper, Monterey jack, sopapillas, apple, and zucchini," he announced at a recent dinner. Later, he told me, "We say 'apple.' But we took butter, vanilla, lemon juice, and cooked it at one twenty-eight—at that temperature, you're just opening up the pores to give it a little punch—then we took it out, cooled it, resealed it, compressed it. When you put it on the plate, it's just an apple. And then you're, like, 'Holy crap, this is intense.'"

For someone who makes beautiful-looking food—at a recent dinner, I heard an architecture student say that she'd based models for her thesis on dishes from Wolvesmouth—Thornton treats appearances as beside the point. For a time, when he felt that too much emphasis was being placed on the visuals, he instituted a brownout. "I started making ugly plates on purpose," he says. "Potato purée with a nicely cooked scallop." Of all the dishes I've eaten at Wolvesmouth, the one that lingers for me is among the unloveliest, a puce-colored pile of rabbit meatballs and mushrooms, leaning sloppily against a folded crêpe, in a puddle of yellow sauce: a briny, cool, and sour-sweet concoction made from lobster shell, shallot, vermouth, and tarragon, with a rich zap of lemon-lime curd. The rabbit still had the whiff of trembly, nervous game.

Thornton is thirty and skinny, five feet nine, with a lean, carved face and the playful, semiwild bearing of a stray animal that half remembers life at the hearth. People of an older generation adopt him. Three women consider themselves to be his mother; two men—neither one his father—call him son. Lost boys flock to him; at any given time, there are a couple of them camping on his floor, in tents and on bedrolls. He doesn't drink, smoke, or often sleep, and he once lost fifteen pounds driving across the country because he couldn't bring himself to eat road food. (At the end of the trip, he weighed 118.) It is hard for him to eat while working—which sometimes means fasting for days—and in any case he always leaves food on the plate. "I like the idea of discipline and restraint," he says. "You have to have that edge." He dresses in moody blacks and grays, with the occasional Iron Maiden T-shirt, and likes his jeans girl-tight. His hair hangs to his waist, but he keeps it tucked up in a newsboy cap with cutouts over the ears. I once saw him take it down and shake it for a second, to the delight of a couple of female diners, then, sheepish, return it to hiding. One of his great fears is to be known as the Axl Rose of cooking.

Dining at Wolvesmouth is a dramatic event: nine to twelve elaborately composed courses prepared in an open kitchen a few feet from the table. Thornton stands over a saucepan with his head bowed intently, his hands quick and careful, a sapper with a live one. Between maneuvers, he darts over to the refrigerator, where he posts the night's menu and, next to each course, the time it was served. Every so often, he steals a glance at the diners and makes a small adjustment on his iPhone, turning up the volume on the music to make people lean in if they seem hesitant to talk and turning it down once the social mood has been established. The first time I went, a few weeks after meeting him, there was half a roasted pig's head, teeth in, glistering fiendishly on the counter as a conversation starter for the guests.

The pressure involved in long-form, dinner-party-style cooking is extreme. "That food has to go out," Miles Thompson, a twenty-four-year-old alumnus of Nobu, who did a stage at Wolvesmouth while figuring out his own underground concept, said. "You promised twelve courses, and you only have that one striped bass. There's no server error, no cook error, no 'Here, I'll buy you a cocktail.'" Thornton's menus are three-dimensional puzzles that remain in pieces until the final hours before the guests arrive. "Cooking is creating a big fucking problem and learning how to solve it," he says.

Because Thornton has no apparatus around him—no wall, even, separating the kitchen from the table—his diners can imagine he belongs to them. Without them, they sense, he would not exist. He is particularly beloved among a circle of Asian eaters who call themselves the Panda Clan and Team Fatass, referring to their panda-related Twitter handles and their appetite for food marathons. When he learned that one of them was about to turn forty, he proposed cooking him a forty-course meal to celebrate. It was a typical Wolvesmouth dinner, miniaturized and quadrupled, and served in four hours. Course No. 24: "chicken liver mousse, pickled pear, watermelon radish, brioche, fleur de sel." No. 31: "lobster, celery root remoulade, black sesame, cherry-white soy vinaigrette." Thornton didn't sleep for three days before the event. "I could've designed the menu differently, but I was, like, I gotta prep everything at the very last minute," he told me. The hardest part was trying not to repeat ingredients, given that each course had four or five components and each component had four or five elements. "All of a sudden, you're going through four hundred things," he said. One of the diners, Kevin Hsu, noted on his blog, *KevinEats*, that he ate more courses at the "40 at 40" than at Alinea, Grant Achatz's three-star restaurant in Chicago, where the tasting menu, which usually runs to twenty courses and costs around $200, is one of the most elaborate and extensive in America.

Wolvesmouth is part of a larger dismantling of fine dining. Nowadays, it's not just menus but restaurants themselves that are seasonal, popping up like chanterelles after a heavy rain. Established chefs, between gigs, squat in vacant commercial kitchens. Young, undercapitalized cooks with catchy ideas go in search of drunken undergraduates: gourmet food trucks. Cooks, both trained and not, host sporadic, legally questionable supper clubs and dinner parties wherever they want. You can pay for a meal in a West Hollywood apartment that belongs to a cook who is by day an assembler of mystery boxes on *MasterChef* and whose only oven is of the toaster variety. In New York, there are dinner parties on subway trains. In Austin, they hunt and field-dress wild boar. Often, you prepay for your "ticket" on PayPal. In most cases, these restaurants are underground in name only. Many of them have websites. A few have "underground restaurant" in the URL.

For chefs, being underground means sidestepping regulations they may find onerous. The ban on foie gras was meaningless to Quenioux, who before it took effect said, "We are known to be a little bit rebellious. They can fine me every day." After the ban, he sent me a picture of his fridge, loaded with glass jars full of gorgeous-looking product. "We have been serving foie at most pop up . . . I won't stop," he wrote. "It is my cultural heritage. It is like taking kimchi away from a Korean." Quenioux's itinerant cheese cart, which rivals Robuchon's, occasionally contains crottin, Rove des Garrigues, or Norman Camembert, all of which are made with unpasteurized milk and not aged the sixty days that the FDA insists upon. "We go *around*," he told me. "I cannot say how. I know it's illegal to do so but I don't mind. Some of my cheeses cannot age that much because the taste changes." At CR8, an expensive dinner that attracts a wine-collecting clientele, the chef recently designed an Alexander McQueen–themed meal. The fifth course featured tonka beans, which he had smuggled from Berlin in his backpack. Tonka beans contain a fragrant compound called coumarin—it accounts for their vanilla-like aroma, and their popularity in European ice creams and desserts—which is also found in strawberries, sweet clover, and mown hay. Fermented, it converts to an anticoagulant and causes hemorrhaging, known as "sweet clover disease," in cattle. In 1954, the FDA deemed coumarin dangerous, and banned it as an additive; tonka beans are still on the FDA's list of "Substances Generally Prohibited from Direct Addition or Use as Human Food."

Chefs continued to cook with tonka beans anyway. "We had them until they went on a door-to-door jihad shutting people down who had them," Wylie Dufresne, the chef at WD-50, a highly regarded experimental restaurant in Manhattan, told me. "There was a moment when you were better off having a firearm than a tonka bean." In 2006, the FDA inspected Alinea's spice cabinet and ordered Achatz, who says he had no idea that it was illegal, to remove the offensive bean. The chef at CR8, whose kitchen doesn't exist, didn't have to worry about the feds. His dish involved a length of mushroom-filled puff pastry rolled to resemble a cinnamon stick, and a sabayon made with tonka bean and cinnamon oil. He said the inspiration came to him after looking at a bowl of potpourri in his bathroom.

"Whenever something is forbidden, it automatically gets cloaked in preciousness," he said. "My guests feel special because they get to experience something most people can't or won't."

Thornton uses the freedom that lack of scrutiny confers to offer ingredients that are impractical for most regular restaurants: too expensive (watershield, a kind of Northwestern lily pad), too weird (oak leaves, which he salted and served with pine broth and matsutake mushrooms), too fleeting (fiddlehead ferns, ramps), or too labor-intensive (cured bonito loin, which he shaves by hand). In the hundreds of meals he has prepared, he has only once served chicken meat, and that was for a private dinner, by request. Hanger steak, of which there are only two per cow, is an unthinkable waste; he serves rib-eye cap if he feels like cooking beef. Ideally, diners at Wolvesmouth will try three or four things they've never had before. Sourcing takes days, and Thornton does almost all of it himself.

In order to serve certain wild ingredients, chefs in regular restaurants must evade forest rangers, health inspectors, and, sometimes, the truth. "I'm very specific about sourcing," one prominent West Coast chef, who gathers by hand in places he's not necessarily permitted to but runs an otherwise very proper dining room, said. "But I don't tell our waitstaff where anything comes from. I just say 'nearby.'" In New York, a well-known chef told me that he has offered birds shot by friends upstate to diners who may or may not realize that what they're eating is illegal: because of the USDA's premortem inspection rule, you can't serve wild birds unless they are imported from the UK—which for some reason is allowed—or your hunting buddy happens to be an inspector. The chef said, "We've served whatever we can get our hands on as long as it's something we could use up quickly enough. It's a 'don't ask, don't tell' kind of thing. It's really not that we're trying to get away with something. It's just that we get excited about it and we know that our customer's expecting the greatest level of quality with all of our ingredients." Because of his unofficial status, Thornton can cook game without fear of losing his business. When the actor Jason Biggs shot a passel of pheasants, Thornton aged them for five days, plucked them, and served them to Biggs and his friends with handmade tagliatelle.

Wild products, the foraging West Coast chef told me, have "that frisson of death," which makes them extra delicious. Black trumpets—wizened, ash-gray eaters of the dead—are among Thornton's favorite ingredients. Their color speaks to his macabre side; he prefers to call them by their less common name, "death trumpets." Their smell is faintly sweet; they like the damp and dark and do not gather at the base of trees, as other mushrooms do. To find them, you have to look straight down. Some mushroom-hunters say that searching for them is like trying to find black holes. Others report the best luck finding them when peeing. Thornton sautés and lightly braises them so they keep their bite.

Recently, he got his hands on a few fiddlehead ferns from Oregon. "They're poisonous when they open up," he said, cleaning them carefully in the kitchen sink. "The toxin gets released. They can wreck you. They're, like, hospital poisonous." He served them, one per plate, on a just less intense green backdrop of puréed asparagus: a tight, poised coil. I had known him for a year at this point, and had seen him fastidiously source and prepare many meals. Eating is an act of trust, and I knew him to be a careful person with a great deal of integrity—a stress case, actually. I studied the coil: exactly how open is "open"? I ate around it for a while. I don't remember the moment of deciding to take a bite. I can imagine the concentrated earthy green flavor, slightly bitter, and feel the ropy, muscular texture of something from the forest floor that strains toward light. But the mind plays tricks.

Although investors have approached Thornton with plans for making Wolvesmouth into a household name, he has been reluctant to leave the safety of the den, where he exerts complete control. "I don't want a business partner who's, like, 'You know, my mom used to make a great meat loaf—I think we should do something with that,'" he told me. "I don't necessarily need seventeen restaurants serving the kind of food I do. When someone gets a seat at Wolvesmouth, they know I'm going to be behind the stove cooking." His stubbornness is attractive, particularly to an audience defined by its pursuit of singular food experiences. "He is obsessed with obscurity, which is why I love him," James Skotchdopole, one of Quentin Tarantino's producers and a frequent guest, says. Still, there is the problem of the neighbors, who let Thornton hold Wolvesmouth dinners only on weekends, when they are out of town. (He hosts smaller, private events, which pay the rent, throughout the week.)

But it is clear to Thornton that he has to bring Wolvesmouth into the light. His kitchen has three functioning burners and one small oven. Once, when the gas went off in the building, he prepped an entire Wolvesmouth dinner in a pair of pressure cookers. He has a dehydrator, an ice-cream maker, good knives, and, aside from a new, $3,000 Cryovac machine, nothing beyond what a moderately ambitious hobbyist might own. His version of the Smoking Gun is a gravity bong rigged from a plastic Voss bottle, a rubber stopper, and a head-shop pipe. One night he packed the bowl full of peachwood and lit it—only to discover, as his guests looked around in surprise, that Wolvesmouth's occasional dishwasher had used it for his own herb of choice and forgotten to clean it.

The Wolvesmouth crew is made up mostly of nonprofessionals; Thornton would like to be able to provide them with full-time work, and health insurance. Matthew Bone, a sweet, lugubrious man of six feet four, with tattoos up to his chin, is a painter; he and Thornton like to talk color theory while their girlfriends go out dancing. Andy Kireitov is an out-of-work heavy-metal guitarist from Siberia. Thornton went to high school with the dishwasher. Caleb Chen and Julian Fang came to Wolvesmouth as diners; so did Garrett Snyder, a husky, sweet-faced food writer in his early twenties who tweets as @searchanddevour. Thornton has taught them all to cook, after his painstaking example, slicing padrón peppers open with a razor blade and tweezing out the seeds. Lacking restaurant lingo, his crew members have evolved their own patois: "ramp" for a gentle-sided bowl that looks good for skating, "lifesaver" for one with a broad outer ring.

Only Greg Paz, a quiet, cat-like Filipino–Puerto Rican former skateboarder who serves as sous-chef, has professional experience. He went to cooking school and then worked at "turn and burn" joints before apprenticing himself to Thornton. Snyder likened Wolvesmouth's stature in the underground-dining scene to that of Kogi, the Korean-barbecue food truck. "There was nothing like it before and there's been nothing like it since," he said. "So many people want to be part of it."

One rainy spring day, a few hours before a Wolvesmouth dinner, Thornton stood over a tile fish, a dour, square-headed creature with a mosaic of silvery and mustard-yellow scales along its back. He wasn't yet sure what to do with it. The fish had come from a sushi wholesaler that supplies Nobu and ships choice specimens to Las Vegas and Aspen. "This morning, they called and said, 'Hey, we just got in some tile fish that's insane,'" Thornton told me. "They know with me I don't care what something costs."

The apartment was quiet and dimly lit. Small pelts were draped here and there; a preserved rat bobbed in a jar—a gift from Eva. Over a long dining table hung a mobile that Thornton fashioned from deer ribs and a jawbone he found in Oregon, and some lichen-covered pieces of applewood he once used to make ice cream. (He burned it, cut it, and soaked it in milk for a couple of days to make the base; finished, he said, it tasted like a campfire.) Paz, who, like Thornton, was dressed in dark, slim-fitting clothes and a black apron, cleaned vegetables. "People have this distaste for vegetables," Thornton said. "They're a lot more work. That's why I like cooking them."

After Thornton finished breaking down the fish, I went with him and Paz on a produce run, a fifty-mile round trip to a two-acre farm near the Long Beach airport. Thornton and a chef friend, Gary Menes, had persuaded the farmer to grow fava beans for them. By the time we arrived, it was pouring. Thornton jumped out of the car and spent the next hour ignoring lightning while picking the beans and a few handfuls of kale—only the smallest, purplest leaves closest to the heart. "Rather than getting it at the farmers' market, this is still alive," he said. "It will have that sweetness. This is what the diners want to hear about." He paused. "You couldn't do it in a restaurant." A patch of bronze fennel shivered in the wind. Thornton picked some and, a few hours later, served it with the final savory course: a tender piece of lamb half buried under snippets of cat grass, periwinkle-blue borage blossoms, yellow-foot mushrooms, and cocoa soil. One side of the plate was devoted to a splat of beet-rhubarb *verjus*, darkly clotting. He called it Spring Slaughter.

Thornton rarely has a chance to test dishes, and much of what he makes he has never eaten before. The education of his palate happened paradoxically: exposure to poor food made him hypersensitive to quality. Growing up, in Bullhead City, Arizona, he shopped for government-supplied groceries in the back room at the St. Vincent de Paul thrift shop. "The peanut butter came in a white jar and had the stamp of a peanut on it; we had powdered milk, powdered eggs, canned meat," he says. "I had a lot of bad, so I can detect bad quickly. I can taste it. I know when a piece of meat has been sitting and reheated, because it has the same flavor as that canned meat." The first meal he remembers making, in his grandmother's kitchen, was a turkey-pickle quesadilla, which he sold back to her for seventy-five cents. On Sunday nights, she made chicken-fried steak, fried okra, and collard greens, or white beans with ham hock and yeasty biscuits. In her honor, he sometimes pickles green strawberries or intentionally adds too much yeast when he bakes.

At Thornton's own house, a boarded-up travel trailer in a part of town that his cousin described to me as "the slum of Bullhead," there often wasn't any food at all. His mother, Elesa, and his stepfather, Emmett, would sell their food stamps to buy drugs. When they cooked, it was meth in the back room. In addition to being an addict, Thornton says, Elesa was mentally ill and susceptible to drug-induced paranoia. He remembers that one time when a social worker made her regular visit to the trailer, Elesa was naked on the couch repeating the sentence "I cut up and chop the hamburger meat"—the only thing she said for several weeks—while he watched *Dennis the Menace* on a TV set with the back torn off to expose the wires, in case they housed surveillance equipment. After thirty minutes, the social worker said, "OK, see you next month!" and left. "Why I have such a hard time with 'authority figures' who want to come in and tell me what to do is that they don't *do* anything," Thornton told me.

Emmett, who was covered in neo-Nazi tattoos and boasted to Thornton about having served time in the penitentiary, was violent and cruel. For fun, he would fill a Super Soaker water gun with gasoline and douse Thornton, threatening to light him on fire. He also hit, dragged, and pepper-sprayed him, and zipped him into a sleeping bag, which he filled with cigarette smoke. (Elesa denies that Emmett was abusive, and that she and Emmett used illegal drugs—though he has an arrest record for drug-related infractions.) At fourteen, Thornton, four feet eight and nicknamed Pudge, started lifting weights for baseball. One summer, he grew a foot. He thought about killing his torturer; instead, he planned his getaway.

Waiting till his mother was coming down from a binge and in need of cash, he paid her fifty dollars saved from his lunch money to sign a form, which he told her was a baseball permission slip. In fact, her signature transferred power of attorney over Thornton to his cousins, evangelical Christians in Riverside County, California, who had offered to take him in. He left the house with his bike and the clothes on his back, pretending that he was going to stay at a friend's. "See you Sunday," he told his mother, and never saw her again.

In 2003, Emmett died, from blunt-force head trauma and a possible overdose of methamphetamine, after he and Elesa had been fighting. She was not charged with a crime, but, according to the death investigation, she was "wishy-washy" about what had happened, and asked the firemen who responded to the scene if she had killed him.

Thornton's California cousins lived in a tract home in Menifee, which locals call Dirttown. To Thornton, it was a deliverance to middle-class normalcy. He rode his BMX, bleached his tips, and had a crush on a neighbor girl. When he went over to friends' houses, he spent his time talking to their parents and grandparents. After high school, he took classes at a local community college and worked at a skate-and-snowboarding shop, where he met Paz. He snowboarded at Mammoth and worked the night shift at Costco; because he didn't have a car, he ran to work four miles on the shoulder of the freeway.

Painting was his primary interest, and he considered going to art school, but he changed his mind and applied to Western Culinary Institute, a branch of the Cordon Bleu, in Portland, Oregon. Wendy Bennett, a chef who taught him there, remembers him as being instinctive and original. "There are very few students that come through culinary school that get it on that level, that don't just rotely re-create what the chef made," she told me. "It's like going to a museum and you see a piece of art and it inspires you to make your own art piece. He wasn't afraid of anything." When class let out, in the late afternoon, he jogged forty blocks to Serrato, a Mediterranean restaurant where he'd landed a position after offering to work for free, and learned to prep in one hour what took the other cooks three.

After graduating, Thornton got a job in Las Vegas on the line at Bouchon, the French bistro owned by Thomas Keller, of The French Laundry and Per Se. Thornton worked eighty hours a week for minimum wage. A few months later, his student-loan debt became overwhelming and he left. Eventually, he moved to Los Angeles, and in 2007, through an agency, got a job working for Nicolas Cage and his family as a private chef. While with the Cages, he began to assemble the pieces to build Wolvesmouth: the table, the chairs, china, glasses, and flatware. "I didn't want to do it janky," he told me. He held his first dinners in an apartment near Larchmont Village, where he lived at the time, and then at a house in the Hollywood Hills belonging to the Olympic gold medalist Shaun White, a friend from his snowboarding days. (He cooked White's meal the night before he won gold in the half-pipe in Vancouver, in 2010.) In 2010, he left the Cages, moved to the loft downtown, and started working on Wolvesmouth full-time.

A hundred years ago, before Progressivism introduced food-service regulations to cities, all restaurants were essentially underground. (As soon as there were regulations, people skirted them: Jacob Riis wrote about a sandwich, "two pieces of bread with a brick between," that sat on the bar at a drinking establishment to prove that it was a restaurant and therefore exempt from blue laws.) At the low end, there were taverns, frequently run out of people's houses, where strangers drank and dined communally on whatever the proprietor was making that night. The rich, on the other hand, entertained in formal hotel restaurants, working with the steward to devise intricate meals with musical and literary interludes. The underground restaurant in the twenty-first century reclaims features of both: the raucous dinner with random tablemates, and the self-conscious staging of an elevated social interaction. Michael Hebb and Naomi Pomeroy were originators of the movement, starting a restaurant in their house in Portland, in 2001. Hebb said that he saw an opportunity to "reinvigorate the convivial in this country." Thornton often finds himself still playing host at two in the morning, hours after the last dish has been served and the burners cleaned in full view of the guests.

Pomeroy and Hebb were inspired by an article that Michael

had read about *paladares* in Cuba, and Family Supper, their event, had something of that subversive air. "It was challenging the notion of the restaurant and the limited number of responses to this basic idea of cooking for people and taking their money," Hebb told me. "It wasn't a middle finger to the health department so much as an indie-rock, anybody-can-do-it, DIY call to arms." He designed collapsible tables out of hollow-core doors, and later, when he and Pomeroy moved their catering business to a commercial kitchen and started holding dinners there, built Murphy tables that could disappear into the walls during the inspector's visits. "We'd get sloshy with our guests and do dishes in the morning," Pomeroy said. "It became a thing, like, 'Ooh, I got invited to Michael and Naomi's for dinner.'"

Eventually, they had ten thousand names on their e-mail list and were open for business five nights a week. With the success of Family Supper, Pomeroy and Hebb founded two restaurants in Portland; in spite of their popularity, food costs got out of control and they were forced to sell, losing hundreds of thousands of dollars of their investors' money. Pomeroy recovered by starting another underground, which she ran out of her backyard. There, Pomeroy, who has become a cooking-world star—a *Food & Wine* Best New Chef, a contestant on *Top Chef Masters*— perfected the ideas for her next restaurant, Beast, a twenty-six-seat place where, five nights a week, she cooks whatever she wants. "When major chefs hear about the way I run Beast, they say, 'You've created a chef's dream restaurant, because you don't have to compromise,'" she told me. "What happens when you do a million-dollar build-out is that you have to be open seven days a week, be really high end, and have a million choices, and that may not work in today's economy."

The lessons of the underground are spreading. "Suddenly, diners are along for the ride. You're paying for insight into one very specific idea of what food should be," Kaitlyn Goalen, an editor at the food newsletter *Tasting Table*, says. "Now it's 'If you don't want what we're offering, you can leave.'" Little Serow, in Washington, D.C., was named one of the country's ten best new restaurants by *Bon Appétit* in 2012; there are no choices and no substitutions, and the menu changes every week. Everybody who goes there knows that the food will be super spicy and the music very loud, and it'll cost $45 a head. Payment, the moment in the restaurant ritual that embodies the emotional drama at its core—you please me, I pay—is also being upended. At Next, which Grant Achatz opened after his success with Alinea, you reserve your seat and buy your meal in advance. As at the theater, you can get season tickets. You pay me, I cook.

The goal of this kind of dining is not seduction so much as it is experience. In the name of gathering some more, I went to pHeast, an itinerant underground restaurant that bills itself as "live art." Isaiah Frizzell, the chef at pHeast, is an amateur molecular gastronomist and a grandson of the honky-tonk singer Lefty Frizzell. "A lot of people claim to be the sons, daughters, and grandchildren of Lefty, but I have his ring in my pocket," he told me. We were standing at a tiny counter in the tiny kitchen of an architect's apartment in Santa Monica. On the floor was a sweating canister of liquid nitrogen. On the counter were deli cups filled with Seussian blobs of green-pea purée that had been spherified with sodium alginate and calcium lactate. "The skin on it creates a gusher inside," he said, depositing the blobs into bowls. They kept bursting. "It's OK, it's OK, if it's gone it's OK," he said nervously. "You still get the effect 'cause you get the gel for the skin."

Frizzell went out to the patio, where the guests were assembled at a long table. "This is nose-to-tail eating, in a vegetable fashion," he said, presenting the peas. Several courses followed, meager and mainly protein-free. At a certain point, even the hostess's enthusiasm seemed to be growing forced. "It is totally amazing what you can do with my tiny kitchen!" she chirped, over a plate of red-cabbage juice that had been turned into what Frizzell described as a "fluid gel" thickened with a tapioca starch. When a tray of bacon-infused whiskey cotton-candy pops, made by the bartender, came around, the diners snatched at them desperately. Then it was time for "nitrogen play." Luckily, one of the other diners was an emergency-room surgeon.

Frizzell decanted the liquid nitrogen into a small bottle with red-bell-pepper coulis and whippits inside, and shook it wildly before shooting the contents into a bowl. Cold smoke tumbled out and rolled down the long table. "Red-bell-pepper Dippin' Dots!" Frizzell announced triumphantly, spooning a pile onto every plate. They melted on my tongue—the ghost of nourishment. I thought of something the founder of a reservation site for underground dining had said about the industry. "We liken it to going to a doctor," she told me. "You don't say, 'This is the medicine I need.' They tell you what you need. The chef tells you what you should be eating." In this case, I was able to self-diagnose: what I needed was some food. I saw a gourmet truck on the way home and stopped for a hot dog.

The traditional restaurant business, with its expensive leases and fickle clientele, can be unforgiving. In the spring of 2007, Gonpachi, an izakaya-style place popular in Tokyo—scenes from *Kill Bill* were filmed there—came to Beverly Hills. It had three buildings and a large garden with a koi pond, and occupied thirteen thousand square feet on a stretch of La Cienega Boulevard. The build took three and a half years and cost more than $18 million. The beams in the main space, a two-story room meant to evoke a traditional village during a festival, were from a nineteenth-century house in Japan. Gonpachi offered sushi, yakitori, and sumiyaki, and had a glass-walled room where patrons could watch a soba master making noodles by hand. In the winter of 2011, it closed.

It was still sitting vacant the following June when Thornton and his crew found themselves with 2,500 servings of food and nowhere to serve it. An event that Dos Equis had planned to throw in an old Bank of America building downtown, with Thornton cooking (and belly dancers, Chinese acrobats, and Brazilian Carnival dancers performing), had been canceled that morning because of a problem with a permit. With half a day's notice, Thornton decided to pop up at Gonpachi.

When I arrived at Thornton's apartment in the late afternoon, I found him in an inside-out green army shirt and his camouflage cap, counting and quartering grilled peaches for a pork-belly dish. "This is a good opportunity to make some people happy who have never eaten the food," he said. The menu—eight courses, designed for a broader spectrum of the beer-drinking public and meant to be consumed in just twenty minutes—was the diffusion version of Wolvesmouth. "I'm trying to appeal to foodies with the technique and consistency but also to have a hook to bring in a mass audience," he had told me earlier. He went over to the fridge, where a menu was posted, and crossed out items that were completed. "Peach done," he muttered. "Tuna done. Tomato relish done. The rib eye we might be able to cook whole. Strawberry. *Tres leches* done. Done done done done done. Finishing fritter. Relish done."

At the dining table, Julian Fang, a heavyset Chinese-American man who is the slightly forbidding keeper of the Wolvesmouth e-mail list, leaned over an Apple computer. Beside him was another computer, a Dell, for his day job as a strategic-account manager at AT&T. He was trying to multitask, and his forehead was covered in sweat. He had written an e-mail to alert the list to the change of plans: the first two hundred to respond would be let into Gonpachi, starting at seven o'clock. The food would be free.

"Is that e-mail sent out?" Thornton asked.

"I can't get anything out of my outbox," Fang said. "It's three fifty-eight p.m. For the love of God, get this thing out!"

The e-mail finally sent, and ten minutes later Thornton peered over Fang's shoulder and said, "We're already half full. Crap." He laughed.

By six o'clock, Thornton and his crew had convened at

Gonpachi, and were exploring the kitchen, with its array of burners, ovens, fridges, sinks. Amid the bounteous wreckage, they set up a survivalist kitchen: a fryer to make cheddar fritters, a circulator to *sous-vide* the pork belly. Thornton ran his hand along the *omakase* bar, disturbing a thick layer of dust. "If I had just this, like, permanently, I would be the happiest guy on the planet," he said.

Thornton showed Caleb Chen how to assemble his dish: corn soup with mole, lime gelée, and cotija cheese, designed to change from sweet to salty to sour to spicy in your mouth. To Fang, he said, "Tuna, lingonberry, lime, black sesame, bok choy." He taught Garrett Snyder how to fan a stack of paper cocktail napkins with the back of his wrist.

The sky darkened and the smell of searing meat filled the garden. Lights came on in stone lanterns and the koi gulped at bubbles on the pond's surface. When the diners started to arrive, Thornton was still putting plastic forks out on the tables. He hurried back to the *omakase* bar and started slicing pork belly. "That gelatinous texture you sometimes get with pork belly doesn't necessarily translate, so I wanted to do a more porky texture that people are used to," he said. A crowd of foodies gathered around. One of them, a recent college graduate, told me that he worked at his aunt's software company, a job he despised, to finance his hobby. In the previous six months he had made two trips to New York, strictly to eat. On the first, he spent five nights in the city and went to eight restaurants, including Daniel and Le Bernardin, each of which has three stars from Michelin; on his second trip, a weekender, he had the extended menu at

Per Se. During the same six months, miraculously, he had lost eighty pounds, due to a running regime and abstemiousness between sprees.

Matthew Selman, the *Simpsons* writer who cast Marge, Lisa, and Bart as food bloggers, leaned toward the bar. "I almost offered you our backyard," he told Thornton, as his wife, a willowy redhead, looked at him querulously. "Renee's given me permission to leave the marriage to eat," he said. "She eats gluten-free bread." The first trays of food went out and disappeared three seconds later. "Are these the guys that cook at Wolvesmouth?" a woman asked her date. "No," her date replied scornfully. "Wolvesmouth is not a *restaurant*."

A hundred and fifty people showed up. At the end of the night, Chen said, "That felt like *Top Chef.* You're thrown into a space and it's, like, 'Now find some stuff to use.' We're so used to a home kitchen that we're, like, 'Oh, my God, what do you do with all this equipment?'" Thornton emerged from behind the bar. He looked a little stunned. "All I had was part of a sandwich today," he said. "I'm wiped." But he was happy. He'd talked to someone who'd been trying to get into Wolvesmouth for two years.

One late-summer evening, Thornton held a Wolvesmouth dinner at his apartment. Fang had his hands in a bowl of bitter steamed black-sesame cake, as porous as volcanic rock. He ripped it into pieces, which he placed on lifesavers lined up along the counter. "Smaller," Thornton said, looking over his shoulder. "We want one big one and one small, so it looks like two mountains." Thornton added chunks of compressed melon;

they glowed like moonstones. He walked the length of the counter flicking lime curd from a metal bowl so that it pooled at the base of each mountain. "Saucing takes a confident stroke," he said. "It's messy without being messy. There's a feel you have to have, like being able to paint."

Matthew Bone stood nearby, moping. He was on day ten of a two-week raw vegan cleanse. He watched a plate sail past. "It kills me that he's making something and I don't know how it tastes," he said. He wrapped two cherry tomatoes in a piece of lettuce and took a big bite. "He never makes the same fucking flavors twice," he said. "They're rainbows. You can't catch them."

When I was twenty-four, my father died in a blind, hunting snow geese on an island in the Rio Grande. At home in suburban Maryland, in the basement where he kept guns locked in a huge steel safe the size of an upright man, we unpacked the duffel from that last trip: dark green, trimmed with tobacco-colored leather, sturdy, simple, well made. Inside, like outlines, were his waders and his crushed boots. There was a small silver flask, half filled with whiskey. My older brother, one of my sisters, and I each took a swig, and said good-bye. The elk that remained in the freezer fed us for years.

The first time I killed an animal, and there haven't been that many, my father dipped his finger in the blood and wiped it on my forehead. It's a rite that properly takes place between fathers and sons. One Thanksgiving, he made his three daughters necklaces from ivory elk canines—the teeth of six animals he had shot, over six seasons—strung with turquoise-colored beads he'd carefully picked out at Beadazzled in Dupont Circle, an image I treasure almost as much as the necklace. He left all of us with more, and more whimsical, taxidermy than you might care to envision. My friends used to take mushrooms just to watch the animals "talk." One of my favorite installations, a small, fierce honey badger—Pepé Le Pew, with fangs, mounted next to a fake fern—commanded particular respect from the handyman of my New York apartment building. I told him how a honey badger can take down a Cape buffalo by attacking its balls; after that, the grouchy, scarce super always got back to me right away. Tufts of fur, brass bullet shells, and pheasant feathers; pieces of skull, skin, and bone: that's what I call interior décor.

At Grant Achatz's Next, the menu is thematic, often historical, and changes four times a year: Paris 1906, traditional Japanese *kaiseki*. This past winter, the menu was "The Hunt." I couldn't resist it, and flew to Chicago to eat. I invited my mother, who lives in St. Louis. During ten years of marriage to my father; she had been handed her share of pheasants to hang.

Next is a windowless space in the West Loop, a meatpacking district that is being overtaken by culinary experiments. Its neighbors are Moto and iNG, restaurants belonging to Homaro Cantu, an inventor, cook, and consultant to industrial food companies. In a lab at Moto, he worked on making a vegan egg, and, in a closet-like "farm" off the kitchen, he grows his own microgreens, square watermelons, and heirloom tomatoes. iNG is devoted to taste-tripping with miracle berry, a West African fruit containing a protein that temporarily tricks the tongue into perceiving sour as sweet, which Cantu believes can alleviate world hunger and reduce carbon emissions by encouraging people to eat otherwise unpalatable plants. iNG's menus are double-designed, to taste like one thing before you eat the berry, and another altogether when the berry is in effect.

At Next, you are not a diner eating in a restaurant, you are an actor in a play about food. We took our seats. Over the white tablecloth the spotted pelt of a fawn was draped; before me was an eighteenth-century sterling walnut pick. "This is a rare opportunity to experience the flavors of the wild—foraged plants, hunted meats, offal—the more primal sensations that we don't get to encounter in our supermarkets," the waiter said. The menu would explore the hunt as an evolutionary necessity and a cultural artifact, from the prehistoric thrill of searing meat on a hot stone to the aristocratic indulgence of eating game from gilded plates.

A glass jewel box with brass hardware was placed on the pelt, steamy and green, a Kew Gardens in miniature. The waiter gave us each a wooden bowl and filled it, from a teapot, with maitake mushroom consommé. "Flip the lid," he said. I was preoccupied with the consommé, a salty, beefy, deep liquor I had to stop myself from drinking in one shot, and didn't hear him. "If you would, *flip the lid.*" The box held two roasted maitake mushrooms, surrounded by snippets of herbs and a roasted onion. "Eat only the mushrooms out of the terrarium," the waiter said. As soon as he was gone, we stabbed the onion with our walnut picks and devoured it, too.

A tall, skinny server with a bushy red beard and a winking aspect slipped my mother a flask curved to fit a hip. "A wee bit of brandy to keep a hunter warm," he said. She waited a second, adjusting to the weird order of events—armagnac with the second course—and asked for something to pour it in.

"Oh! Did you want a glass?" He appeared genuinely confused. "The intention is to taste it out of the flask." She blushed and did what he said. The charcuterie—rabbit pâté, elk jerky, wild boar salami, blood sausage, venison-heart tartare—was served on disks of deer antler, set into a sap-oozing log. There were tiny deep purple hibiscus leaves grown in Ohio by Farmer Lee—he of the trademarked overalls—and caviar from sturgeon "wild-caught in the Caspian, then farm-raised in Florida."

A silver candelabra appeared, and was lit: time to play nobility. Here came a cold course of woodcock, served with cocoa powder, black truffles, and a tangle of gold leaf. On one side of the plate was a dab of sauce made from hazelnuts and huckleberries, a culinary diorama that was the equivalent of a fake fern for a stuffed badger.

The next course was squab—baby pigeon—with all its parts, and offal en croute. The head, bisected, lay beside a fan of breast. At the edge of the plate was a talon. "Let's see if they eat it," the woman at the table next to us said. She and her husband hadn't; their grown kids, sitting across from them, had. I picked up the bird by the convenient tweezer of its beak and licked out the garlic-and-parsley-soaked brain. This time I was untroubled by the brain; maybe I have a mammalian prejudice. Or maybe I was seduced by surface: this plate was supremely beautiful, its challenging elements aestheticized. A stagehand, dressed in black, sweeping, stopped and whispered to us, "When Chef

Morimoto"—the Iron Chef—"was here, there were no bones left on the plate."

It was an art-historical exegesis of a meal, with fifteen color plates. I have no idea what it might have meant to anyone else. For me, it was like feasting on my past. The smoky old flavors overwhelmed me, like a dream about a ghost that leaves you sad in the morning. I gnawed the meat from the talon, leaving the grip at the end of a spindly bone, the shrunken remains of a vanquished witch. My father would have made something fabulous from it. I almost put it in my purse. But in fairy tales purloined things have a way of turning into dust.

CODA

It was Easter week. My baby had just said her first word, "duck." Jonathan Gold was busy, doesn't much like Filipino food, and, besides, is afraid of eggs. Abby Abanes—who *is* Filipina—thinks *balut* is gross. I decided to face this beast on my own. It wasn't that I had a "list"; it was a personal test. I was curious, both about what it would taste like, and about whether I could stomach it. I thought of all the challenging things I had eaten over the past few years. How bad could it be? Maybe I would even like it.

I looked on Yelp and started calling. Nobody had it. Finally, I tried a place called Bahay Kubo, near downtown, run by someone with the perfectly discomfiting name Mommy Lucing. *"Balut?"* The woman who answered the phone said. "Come tomorrow at eleven."

The next morning, as the hour approached, I dawdled

around the house. I hadn't meant to go there hungry, but, stall
ing, let the morning slip by, and now it was lunchtime. I got in
the car, and eventually I found myself driving in a part of the
city I had first come to with Gold. There was Langer's, the pastrami place, and Mama's, where we went for tamales. I had my
bearings. Passing MacArthur Park, I drove up a steep hill,
around a corner, and into an unfamiliar Filipino pocket. Next
to an apartment complex called Manila Terrace was a low
building with a green awning and a Philippine National Bank
Rapid Remit center. There was an "A" in the window.

Everyone inside was Filipino. A bamboo shanty on the
patio housed a large TV; the TV inside was larger, and tuned to
a Filipino talent show. The service was cafeteria-style, which
meant I could talk to the lady behind me in line. "Don't eat
that," she said, scrunching up her nose, when I told her I wanted
to try *balut*. "What, you like feathers?" She cut me in line and
left me on my own.

When it was my turn to order, I asked the man behind the
counter for taro leaves in coconut milk. He was middle-aged
and wore a tight red shirt, a white belt, and a diamond stud in
his ear. "I don't think you're going to like it," he said, and made
me taste it before he would put it on my plate. He was wrong,
though. It was an island version of creamed spinach—bitter,
rich, and sweet—and I liked it fine.

On top of the glass partition separating customers from the
food was a small foam box secured with red, green, and yellow
tape. A sign attached to it said *"Balut, $1.85."* "One of those,"
I said. Red Shirt raised his eyebrows, opened the box, and
handed me a bluish-green duck egg, still warm, that fit in the

palm of my hand. "Crack it, drink the juice, and then close your eyes," he said. At the checkout, I asked for a 7-Up. If they'd sold ginger ale, I would have ordered that, remedy of childhood.

I carried my tray to a green faux-marbled table and sat down. Taking a bite of rice, I noticed that I was actually shaking. I cracked the bottom of the egg and peeled a little. Red Shirt had come out from behind the counter and was hovering around. "Wrong end," he said. I kept going, chipping off pieces of shell. They were espaliered with dark red blood vessels. I had never seen this before. An unfertilized egg has no need of circuitry. I put my lips up to the hole I'd made and drank the liquid, a nice light chicken broth, then peeled some more, until I saw yolk.

I picked up a white chunk. In my mouth, I felt it give way into dark reddish brown meat. I didn't need to take it out to examine it, I could see it with my tongue: my first and worst possible experience of synesthesia. I felt like a sharp-toothed animal, burrowing for meat. From my mouth, I pulled what was apparently a fingernail trimming. Meanwhile, I had to do something about the rest of the bite. Staring at nothing, keeping a bead on the talent show from the corner of my eye, like a seasick person trying to get steady, I swallowed.

I looked down at my tray. There, in the half shell, was a small creature, nestled into itself, a glazed eye, a billow of nourishing yolk. That is, *part* of a small creature.

"You should eat it all at once, if you can do it," Red Shirt said, and handed me a shaker of salt.

Eating a creature and its food: aren't whole lifestyles built on avoiding that? And isn't foodie culture obsessed with artificially creating it? I thought of Cosentino's pig and watercress, Achatz's huckleberry and woodcock. I was a third of the way there. Why turn back now. I stole a sip of 7-Up and I took another bite. The familiar, not unpleasant taste of organ meat.

"It makes you strong," Red Shirt said. "It's the Filipino Viagra. It's like eating an oyster." I couldn't believe it—this darkest, most poignant maternal food, this was for men, too? I pulled the last piece of meat from the shell, determined to finish. This was a big bite, but I was almost there. Chewing, I hit an inexplicable texture, like a soft tooth. Single-minded, I mashed it to a paste and braced myself to swallow. Just as I was congratulating myself, thinking it was a mental game and I had won, something terrifying happened. From a deeper place than my taste buds—they could be tricked by a lick of chicken soup—rebellion. I felt a shift in my upper stomach, a violent bubbling, and the beginnings of a catastrophe.

Acknowledgments

I owe an incalculable debt of gratitude to *The New Yorker*, in particular to David Remnick, who has encouraged me at every turn; Dorothy Wickenden, a champion and a friend; and Nick Trautwein, a singularly gifted reader and collaborator. I want to thank Sarah McGrath for providing the spark and the fuel, and all the other thoughtful, smart people at Riverhead. Eric Simonoff for gracious stewardship. Stacey Kalish and Lila Byock for many meaningful contributions. Eliza Griswold, Claire Hoffman, Meghan O'Rourke, and Kevin West for reading and re-reading. Lila again, Eric Mercado, and Nate Stein for double-checking me.

I want to thank my mother for her curiosity, perceptivity, and steel trap. You inspired this.

To the people who let me into their kitchens, met me for

dinner, talked to me when they had other things that needed to be done: thank you. Your stories make the book.

My deepest thanks go to my husband, Billy, for supporting and sustaining me, and to our children for bringing me endless happiness.